FRANKIE ~~~~~~ MY HAMSTER

FRANKIE VAUGHAN ATE MY HAMSTER

Growing up in the East End

Rikki Brown

BLACK & WHITE PUBLISHING

First published 2011
by Black & White Publishing Ltd
29 Ocean Drive, Edinburgh EH6 6JL

1 3 5 7 9 10 8 6 4 2   11 12 13 14

ISBN: 978 1 84502 337 9

A CIP catalogue record for this book is available from the British Library.

The stories in this book are about real people and events. Where appropriate,
some names and places have been changed to respect privacy.

Typeset by Iolaire Typesetting, Newtonmore
Printed and bound by MPG Books Ltd, Bodmin

CONTENTS

For Lucy and Joshua

FOREWORD

BY IAN PATTISON

Frankie Vaughan never ate Rikki Brown's hamster. To even suggest such a thing, let alone to assert it as an incontrovertible fact, is a grotesque, despicable outrage of the most contemptible order. Mr Vaughan was, over many decades, an illustrious pillar of the British entertainment establishment. I am proud to say I knew Frankie personally and very seldom did I ever see him eat a hamster. And even then never before a performance. True, once the hits had dried up, he turned to consuming small rodents – voles, squirrels (grey, never red), white mice and guinea pigs – but this was purely comfort eating and must be viewed compassionately, in the forgiving context of an extended career lull. After all, who among us has not treated a small animal inappropriately during a time of acute personal crisis?

I knew Rikki Brown and I knew his hamster. In truth, I preferred the hamster. Rikki Brown and the bewitching 'Hammie' first came to my attention when I was working at the BBC Scotland Entertainment Department, which was located then in the crypt of Glasgow Cathedral. When Hammie hopped onto my desk and started using my pencil sharpener as an exercise wheel, it was evident, straight away, which of the two had the charisma.

Rikki worked his gifted hamster pitilessly. It was Colonel Parker and Elvis all over again, except that Elvis, to our knowledge, never played St Mary's Borstal.

As the money rolled in, so Rikki indulged his taste for exquisite artworks and added to his glittering collection of satellite dishes. The walls of his home were adorned with original works by his favourite artists, Burberry, Kappa and B&Q. But it was never enough and Rikki, as the creative engine room of the double act, felt horribly overshadowed . . .

How Hammie the hamster died will remain forever a showbiz mystery. Some say drug overdose and others millet overdose. It is known she suffered recurring weight problems and by her demise had ballooned to a curvaceous fourteen ounces. At her funeral, Rikki Brown's grief was ostentatious. Wearing a white tuxedo, he threw a single lettuce leaf into her coffin before disappearing to Polmont to mourn his loss with two vivacious young pole-dancing twins, Arthur and Tommy Cheeves. For some, the finger of suspicion remains pointing inexorably in his direction.

And now, at last, Rikki Brown has written his early memoirs. Will he speak truthfully of the murky events surrounding the death of his beloved hamster? My advice is simple: Read the lines; then read between the lines; finally, dig up the lines and peer under them using a strong torch. Beneath the dusty litter of Rikki Brown's discarded jokes, lies the truth. 'Lies the truth.' See what I did there?

Here's Frankie Vaughan with 'Mr Moonlight'.

PREFACE

People often ask me if I ended up working in comedy because at school I used humour as a defence against bullying. The answer is an emphatic 'no'. For me humour was the worst defence against being bullied because whenever I made a comment that I thought would defuse a situation it was met with a 'so you think you're funny do you?' and I'd get beaten up. I'd like to add that I still hate bullies and bullying is never, ever an acceptable practice. Unless, of course, you went to school with Jedward.

RB

1

GROWING UP IS HARD TO DO

The thing I remember most about my preschool years is that I was always heavily armed. Every birthday and Christmas I received a toy gun because all previous generations of my family had been to war. So the earlier I learned to handle a firearm, the better chance I had of survival when it came to handling the real thing for Queen and Country.

In the final scene of Al Pacino's movie *Scarface*, a team of hit men from a Columbian drugs cartel are invading his estate and to defend himself he opens up a cupboard to reveal an array of assault rifles, hand guns, rocket launchers and machine guns. My reaction to the scene was: 'Call that a weapons cupboard? When I was four my toy cupboard was twice that size.' Pacino's character, Tony Montana, waved his assault rifle about menacingly with the line, 'Say hello to my little friend.' When I waved my rifle about, my line was, 'Say hello to just a very small sample from my very vast arsenal.'

However, as I was four during the Cuban missile crisis none of the arms I possessed would have been much good against the threat at that time, which wasn't Columbian drugs cartels but the Russians and their intercontinental ballistic missiles. A toy Winchester rifle versus nuclear oblivion. The Russkies would probably have had the upper hand in that little skirmish.

Not that being targeted by a nuclear missile would have bothered Glaswegians much because their reaction would have been, 'I've had worse burns affa sitting too close to a three bar

1

electric fire,' and, 'Radiation poisoning? Naw I think it was the donner kebab I had on top of sixteen pints.'

Evidently being nuked was a real worry back then, so much so that the government produced a leaflet called *Protect and Survive* that was delivered to every household. It was full of handy hints on how to survive the nuclear Armageddon. Basically, take a door off its hinges, lay it against a wall, pile furniture against it and hide behind the door with a radio, a torch and a bucket for a toilet. I suppose the government had to do something, so *Protect and Survive* was the something they did. Seems they realised that a more honest and truthful publication called *You're Fucked* might have induced panic.

As it transpired my generation didn't have to go to war unless we wanted to because the days of getting a letter saying, 'Dear Cannon Fodder, you have won the opportunity to get shot at, love, The Government,' were over. This meant the long, long tradition of members of my family fighting in Korea, World War Two, World War One, the Boer War, the Zulu War, etc, etc, ended with me. I say me, but I did have one uncle who was a conscientious objector and the closest he ever got to serving in the military was when he worked as John Mills's lighting stand-in in *The Colditz Story*. My granny on my father's side lost three brothers in World War One, so as far as I was concerned if there was a war I wasn't going because my family had more than done their bit.

Up until the age of four I was brought up in Corkerhill in a village that had been purpose built at the back of Pollok Park by British Rail to house railway workers and their families. Most of the families who inhabited the village moved up to Glasgow from Carlisle just after World War One, my grandparents on my mother's side amongst them.

After World War Two there were a few families with Italian fathers because during that war Pollok Park contained an Italian POW camp to house the prisoners who were made to work on the railway. Many of them remained after the war, married local girls and swapped forced labour with British Rail for paid labour with British Rail. Not a bad deal.

Corkerhill was row after row of quaint red brick houses with indoor toilets. I mention the indoor toilets because this was a big deal back in the 1920s and anyone who had an indoor lavatory was considered posh, much in the same way today that anyone who mentions they've got a bidet is considered posh. Having no inside toilet must have been a nuisance; this modern generation can say, 'I'm off to the bog, back in a minute,' while in the twenties they said, 'I'm off to the bog, where's my coat, shoes and the stick for wedging against the lavvie door to keep it shut, back in half an hour, because it is a two mile walk after all.'

I don't remember much about my Papa (Papa is an English thing for grandfather) other than he drove a steam train and hated Winston Churchill because he thought he was a war-monger. It's funny because you'd think everyone of that generation would have loved him because he saw off Hitler. But they didn't.

I don't actually have that many memories of my time in Corker-hill because I was obviously very young but the ones I do have are of feeding chickens and being perpetually covered in soot because it was the age of coal-powered steam locomotives and our house was about forty yards from the railway sheds. But the one memory I recall the most is of two dogs going at it in the street, and when I say going at it I mean they were doing 'it', in fact they were so busy doing 'it' that they didn't notice that a crowd had gathered to cheer them on. My mother told me they were dancing. At four you'll believe anything. But the main reason this stuck in my head was that they were separated by a neighbour throwing a bucket of water over them. I thought, 'Wow, they're tough on dancing round these here parts.' Corkerhill, I wrongly assumed, was the Scottish equivalent of the Midwest-USA, bible-bashing small town that Kevin Bacon moved to in *Footloose*.

Corkerhill was indeed quaint and also very charming in a ye-old-worlde-model-village kind of a way. It had greenhouses,

wash houses and its own town hall, and if Glasgow Corporation, as was, hadn't bulldozed it flat in the 1960s, it would now
be one of the city's main tourist attractions. I don't know what
Glasgow Corporation were up to but they practically levelled
the city. You do hear about local government corruption, which
begs the question: just how many shares in bulldozer companies
did the councillors actually have? It must have been millions.

My parents and I lived in one room in my grandparent's
house, which wasn't ideal but houses were at a premium in the
fifties and sixties and my parents were on a long list for their
own house. The one room scenario wasn't helped much by the
fact that my parents had the first TV in Corkerhill and, small
though it was, it took up most of the room. The lack of space was
made even worse by the constant stream of visitors who came to
gawk in awe at whatever was on. Gawk in awe? Wasn't that the
tactics the Americans adopted in the Gulf War?

The TV wasn't bought but rented from Radio Rentals. No one
bought a TV as they were so expensive, and being under a rental
contract meant that when it broke down Radio Rentals sent a
man to repair it. TVs broke down frequently, so much so that I
ended up calling the man who came to replace the valves every
other week Uncle Frank. The only kids programming available
was on the BBC's *Watch With Mother* series, which was on at
1.30pm every weekday for fifteen minutes.

My favourite was *The Woodentops*, according to my Mother
anyway. I recall Spotty Dog, but that's it. Thinking back I'm
pretty sure my favourite wasn't *The Woodentops* but *Tales from
the Riverbank* with live Hammy the Hamster and Roderick the
Rat who travelled around the waterways of Britain on a small
toy boat. I suspect that they didn't really travel willingly and
their feet were glued to the deck of the boat because the director
didn't want them to escape or fall off the boat and drown.

The other options were Bill and Ben of *The Flower Pot Men*,
Rag, Tag and Bobtail and *Andy Pandy*. I may have been four at the
time, but even at the age of four I thought Andy Pandy was a

dick. We did have *Sooty*, too, I suppose but he was just as annoying as you couldn't understand a word he was saying. In his defence, who would be articulate with Harry Corbett's hand stuck up their backside?

In 1961 my parents' dreams finally came true and they received a letter offering them a house in the newly built scheme of Easterhouse. Okay, perhaps dream is maybe the wrong word for it considering what was to come, because who knew in 1961 that a few years later Easterhouse would have become the bench mark for utterly incompetent social planning? The social planners must have been off Social Planning College the day they covered providing even the most basic facilities.

The home we were offered was at 45 Wardie Road. It was a bright red sandstone close of six flats but the council didn't allocate any particular flat and the one you ended up in was decided by a council housing officer with a cloth bag containing six sets of keys. Lots were drawn to see whose hand went into the bag first and the set you picked decided the house you'd get. As I recall, my Dad was the third chooser and he picked top right, which was considered a premium pick. You didn't want the bottom flat because bottom flats are easy to break into and you had someone above you and that could be noisy, and you didn't want the middle flat for the latter reason, but the top, that was burglar proof and with no one above you, you were the ones who could be noisy for the tenants below.

We moved in to the house in January after my last Christmas in Corkerhill. A Christmas I remember in great detail because every previous Christmas I woke up to two pillow cases full of weapons, but at Christmas 1961 I woke up to just one. 'Hey, excuse me, I think there's been some sort of mix up here.' It was no mix up. On 19 December my brother Martin had been born and my arsenal allowance had been halved, forever. To say I was pissed off was probably an understatement and I couldn't have been hiding it very well because my Nana (calling your Granny a Nana is also an English thing) tried to soften my disappointment by telling me that all she ever got for Christmas was an apple, an orange and a penny. I don't recall my reaction to that but it was more than likely a sarcastic, 'Aye, so ye pure did.'

I also remember that year because my Nana took me to see Santa in Lewis's department store in Argyle Street and I had my photograph taken sitting on Muffin the Mule. I came across this photograph again when I was twelve and I showed it to my mates, a couple of whom were older at about fifteen and one of them said, 'Muffin the Mule, that's a sexual offence.' Being twelve and naive I had absolutely no idea what he was talking about. When I was nineteen I was less naive and it was a case of, 'Aw, right, I get the Muffin the Mule joke now, that's quite funny.' Seven years to get a joke leads me to believe that I'm the last person a stand up comedian would want in his audience.

Every year Santa would arrive at Lewis's in a big Christmas parade along Argyle Street and there would be a huge throng of parents and kids, and drunks. Most of them were still drunk from the Orange parade six months previously. The parade was led by a marching band who ignored the occasional shouts of, 'Gies "The Sash",' which were usually followed by, 'Naw, well, get it right up yeez then,' when they continued to play 'Santa Claus Is Coming To Town'. I think I was taken to see Santa up until I was maybe eight or nine because somewhere in between I stopped believing he was real since he didn't bring the Scalextric set I'd asked him for. I did eventually get Scalextric, from my parents, but it was rubbish and nowhere near as exciting as it was portrayed in the adverts. At every bend the car flew off the track. Total rubbish, and in my opinion it's not too late for the Advertising Standards Authority to launch a full and thorough investigation into the claims of the 'ultimate in excitement'. Santa-wise the early sixties were a different time because most parents now wouldn't pay for their kids to sit on a man's knee unless the department store erected a certificate behind Santa assuring them that he wasn't on the sex offenders register. Back then it was, 'On you go, you'll be fine, he's not really that drunk.'

2

A NEW LIFE

So, there we were in 1962 as we flitted and began our new life in Easterhouse in a close that comprised of the Hairs, the McDonalds, the McPhersons, the Davidsons, the Connors and the Browns. The McPhersons were only there for six months before emigrating to Australia for £10 with an assisted passage and they were replaced by the Petersons. The mother was a bit strange because she never opened her door and would talk to any callers through the letterbox. Every time anyone went to their door it was like trying to get into a Speakeasy.

We hadn't been there very long when Mormon missionaries started appearing in the area. The fact that the Mormon Church in Salt Lake City deemed Easterhouse an area in need of missionaries was surely a bad omen but no one put two and two together at the time. They were very clean cut and immaculately dressed, and were also willing to answer questions. In the early sixties the questions were along the lines of, 'Are youse mental?' and in the early seventies the questions were always along the lines of, 'Do you know the Osmonds?' Who knows, maybe some of them were the Osmonds. Given how many Osmonds there are, there was every likelihood that their number did indeed include the toothy ones. It must have been a pretty pointless exercise for them because everyone in Easterhouse was either a Protestant or a Catholic and had no intention of ever becoming anything else.

The close itself was always kept spotless because, as this was every family in the close's first home, they were proud of it and every mother took their turn of the stairs and the windows. The proud first homeowner thing was one reason it was kept spotless, the other reason was that the biggest insult you could give to a Glasgow woman was to tell her, 'See you, you keep a dirty hoose.'

In the summer of 1962 I was taken into town and kitted out with a school uniform for the start of my education at Wellhouse School. I was bought a blazer that was about seven sizes too big. The shop didn't sell blazers for five-year-olds. There was no point, as they'd never have sold any because to save money most parents, like mine, bought blazers for twelve-year-olds that you'd 'grow into'. Wellhouse was quite far away but a new school was planned and I was only to attend Wellhouse until the new school, Easthall, was built. However, I didn't get to go to school that August, or September or even October. As it turned out I was going to be very late indeed for my first day at school.

As a pre-going-to-school treat my parents had taken me to Calderpark Zoo where I caught Scarlet Fever. This was a death's-door scenario in the early sixties. There were so many diseases that it was practically impossible to get through your childhood without catching something unpleasant. The NHS inoculated us against everything they could think of: diphtheria, tuberculosis, typhoid, measles and, my personal favourite, polio. Not my favourite disease I hasten to add, it was my favourite because immunity didn't involve an injection – it involved being treated like a pony and given a sugar cube.

Despite this, some diseases still got through. However, almost dying of Scarlet Fever and taking a very long time to recover was worth it because I enjoyed the day, as the zoo had good stuff like polar bears and lions. Lions are usually big and brave in the jungle, but this lot spent their entire day looking like they were shitting themselves because they'd found out the council had built Easterhouse a mere couple of miles away from their unnatural habitat. Thinking back, Calderpark Zoo (which eventually became Glasgow Zoo) had loads of animals – wallabies, camels, rhinoceroses, bison and even elephants. I'd seen elephants before at the annual Christmas Circus and Carnival in the Kelvin Hall, although I should perhaps say that I'd smelled elephants before because the whole Kelvin Hall smelt of elephant crap. I defy any Glaswegian who, for whatever reason, comes in contact with the smell of elephant crap and doesn't immediately think 'Kelvin Hall'. The council may have turned it into a transport museum and a sports arena but the Kelvin Hall will always mean elephant shite to me.

Glasgow Zoo eventually closed down but it wasn't an immediate closing, it was a slow painful process as the zoo struggled on with less and less animals until no one really wanted to pay to see the last remaining few – one chimpanzee and a couple of gerbils. When the animals died, the zoo couldn't afford to replace them, but it did beg the question, what happened to the animals that died? How do you dispose of a rhinoceros's body? All I can say is that during the lengthy and painful demise of the zoo there seemed to be a much wider range of meats available at the local snack bar and restaurant.

Scarlet Fever kept me off school for a year, which, as it happened, really wasn't much of a problem because for the first twelve months the entire curriculum involved no more than instructions on using writing implements without getting them stuck up your nose. Now I'm not bragging here, actually I am, but at the end of my spring first term, despite being one year behind everyone else, I came first in the class. Or 'First For General Excellence' as it said in the book I received as a prize. Looking back, maybe I was a genius. Well, it was either that or the rest of my class were effing idiots. This was in 1963/64, a completely, completely, completely different time. I'm labouring the completelies here because the book I received as First Prize for my General Excellence (probably also an understatement) was *Uncle Remus and Brer Rabbit Stories*. A book that nowadays may not be looked upon as completely PC, but it was a different time and you can't go around rewriting old books to suit modern sensibilities just because the very easily offended go out of their way to find something to be offended about in them.

In the early sixties schools still proudly displayed big maps of the world on the walls with the British Empire marked out in red to show just how much better than Johnny Foreigner we the British were. The fact that my First Prize for General Excellence contained some pretty dubious racial stereotyping really wasn't thought of as an issue. Not in an era when the logo for Robertson's Jam was considered no more than the logo for Robertson's Jam. We're now actually a bit embarrassed about the British Empire's role in the world, so embarrassed that the city of Glasgow recently apologised for slavery. Good that they apologised in 2009 because it's best to nip Glasgow's role in the slave trade in the bud before it gets out of hand.

I don't think it was a personal apology because there was no one to apologise to so it was more of a ceremonial PR apology to attempt to take the bad look off 90% of Glasgow's architectural gems being built using the profits from rum, sugar, tobacco and cotton, and Uncle Remus and Brer Rabbit books. What form did the apology take? It was more than likely a council official saying 'Helluva sorry by the way. Here, have a Glasgow's Miles Better t-shirt which I'm sure more than makes up for the whole profiting from the slave trade thing.'

In 1963 I was playing in my bedroom when I heard my mother shout, 'Oh my God! They killed Kennedy.' There had been a newsflash on the telly made by a grim-faced newsreader. In the days before twenty-four-hour rolling news a newsflash was a big deal because it was never good news. The programme you were watching would be interrupted by a newsflash graphic and a man – it was always a man – would appear saying, 'A dead bad thing has happened.' Although in the case of STV, if the news came in during the day, they interrupted their daytime programming, which was only ever a picture of a Scottish scene accompanied by the song 'Charlie Is My Darling' playing on a loop. No matter if you tuned in at 10am or 11am or 12.45pm or 2.13pm, it was always 'Charlie Is My Darling'. Compared to some of the stuff STV broadcast nowadays, 'Charlie Is My Darling' with the countryside scene is practically Bafta Award winning.

In 1968 I was playing in my bedroom as usual when I heard my mother shout, 'Oh my God! They killed Kennedy.' A different Kennedy this time, obviously. Now I'm only guessing here but I think it was my mother's exclamations of shock that inspired *South Park*'s, 'Oh my God! They killed Kenny,' catchphrase. Being six, I was a bit easy oozy about the J. F. Kennedy assassination and watching the footage of the motorcade I didn't think that it was terrible, I just thought 'nice car'.

Primary school is the school we go to where we formulate our early opinions of the world but all I can recall is the teachers perpetually telling us a story concerning the whereabouts of Chicken Licken and Turkey Lurkey. One of the two had a nasty bump on his head, I forget which, and the whole plot centred on where and how he received his injury. What was to be learned from this literary masterpiece still defeats me. Perhaps it was subliminal. We did, I suppose, also have *Janet and John* books and they couldn't have had much influence on me because I can't recollect even slightly what they were about.

We were the post-World War Two generation and we carried our books in what we called haversacks, which were khaki canvas bags that had been previously used to carry gas masks. Probably wouldn't have looked out of place in the biological warfare section of my toy cupboard. We wore a lot of ex-army surplus clothes because they were cheap and hardwearing. It had quite an effect on the school photograph, what with half the class looking like school kids and the other half looking like Chinese generals.

In retrospect I suppose I did learn a lot from those years though. For instance, I could tell a parent's taste in home decor by the wallpaper they'd covered their kid's school books in, and I could tell a fellow pupil's father's income by looking at the price on his or her dinner ticket. If your father had a good job you paid 4/6d a week, not so good a job and 2/6d was printed on your dinner ticket. If your father was amongst the lower paid the price of a weekly dinner ticket was 1/3d and if your father was unemployed you were issued with a free dinner ticket. The Data Protection Act was decades off, so many decades off that not only was your father's income there to be seen by every dinner lady, or anyone within seeing distance, but if your father didn't have a job this could be seen by almost everyone because your free dinner ticket was a different colour from the paid ones.

There was no sensitivity when it came to the nit nurse either. If she found you had nits she'd shave your head. Not completely, but not far off it, and if she found you had impetigo she painted your lips with gentian violet. There was nothing subtle about having your human rights breeched and some pupils returned from the nurse with either a shaved head or bright purple lips, leaving them marked out like a plague victim with a yellow cross on their front door. Children are insensitive and referred to anyone with nits or impetigo as having the 'meegy'. One unfortunate girl in my class whose name was Kim not only had nits and impetigo, but she also had scabies. Kids can be cruel and in this case they were *The Lone Ranger* cruel because she ended up being called Kimo Scabby for the rest of her time at primary.

It wasn't just the three aforementioned inflictions that led to 'meegy' accusations, if your house smelt of cabbage that was a sure sign of 'meeginess' too. Many houses did indeed smell of cabbage and in this age of nostalgic fond memories of the sixties I'm surprised, actually, that no one has invented a smell of cabbage spray to bring the aroma of that era back into the modern age. A cabbage-smelling house was usually a sign of abject poverty and a wholly cabbage-based diet but it was also part of a grand master plan.

Warrant sales were commonplace and many times the Sheriff Officers would turn up and pile up a household's furniture outside the close for sale to scum. There's no other way to describe the vultures who turned up to make a huge profit by buying their belongings for threepence and selling them on with a 10,000% mark up. The grand master plan was to make everything you owned smell of cabbage because no vulture would then want to buy it. Everyone empathised with the victims of warrant sales because the attitude was 'there for the grace of God go I'.

The ladies of the warrant sale houses found it hard to make ends meet, especially because in a lot of the cases they were in debt because the man of the house had drunk away his pay packet. You couldn't consolidate your debts in the sixties – you could only cover your debts by having your wardrobes, chairs and couches sold off by people who were 'only following orders'. It was an excuse that wasn't accepted at Nuremberg and an excuse that wasn't accepted in Easterhouse either. This led the locals to vandalise cars belonging to those involved in executing warrant sales, an act the police turned a blind eye to because they had no love for debt collectors either. It was always the council who set the Sheriff's Officer on people either for non-payment of rent or rates. It was hard if you were poor to get into other debt as you couldn't get credit in the first place. Hire purchase was only available if you could pay a third down on what you were buying, and if you were poor the very last thing you'd have would be a third to put down on white goods. You never saw warrant sales in the well-off areas and people from the richer parts probably didn't even know such a draconian practice existed. Any posh folk who happened to get lost and ended up driving through Easterhouse in their fancy car would have noticed the tables and chairs outside the close and as-sumed that Easterhouse wasn't as bad as people were saying because it has Parisian style street cafes.

Life at school was an endless whirl of egg and spoon races and snotters. The teachers didn't talk to us much, but they did talk at us plenty. In fact, the only time I remember being spoken to directly at Wellhouse was when I was asked if I had a hankie, which was the teacher's way of saying, 'For God's sake boy, wipe your nose.'

Wellhouse was a Protestant school and we had a Catholic school opposite, the name of which was Blessed John Ogilvie. Next to that was an enormous Catholic chapel – the usual sort of enormous Catholic chapel always found in poor areas. Why were the chapels so big and the people so poor? I suspect it was probably something to do with how every Friday night priests and nuns would go round the scheme visiting Catholic families to collect money for the chapel building funds. Why people would prefer having a giant chapel before having food on their table is beyond me.

Blessed John Ogilvie's became St John Ogilvie's when he was canonised after a miracle was attributed to him. I can't remember what the miracle actually was but I think it involved him being prayed to prior to Celtic's match against Inter Milan in the 1967 European Cup Final. The only thing I do know about John Ogilvie I learned from the very accurate and informative website Wikipedia, where it lists him as one of Glasgow's very few Christian martyrs. The reason that Glasgow has very few Christian martyrs is because given the choice between death and changing your mind about something, the average Glaswegian will lump for the mind changing every time. We're not stupid after all, and even if you didn't agree with what you were changing your mind about it doesn't count anyway if you had your fingers crossed behind your back. How could John Ogilvie not know that, and all the other Christian martyrs for that matter?

The other big chapel was St Benedict's and I know even less about St Benedict, but since Benedictine monks make Buckfast I'm guessing he's the Patron Saint of Coatbridge. I was jealous of the Catholic kids because they never seemed to attend school much thanks to days off in the celebration of what seemed like 365 saints. No that's not true, figuring in weekends they must have only had 261 saints because a saints commemoration day never fell on a Saturday or a Sunday as that would just be daft because they were off anyway.

Religion was completely beyond me. I thought it was to do with whichever team you supported. Turns out as I lived in Glasgow I was right. Rangers fans went to Protestant schools, Celtic fans went to Catholic schools and Partick Thistle fans were atheists who were home schooled. What about Clyde fans? No one knew any so it was thought that they didn't actually exist and Clyde and it's fans were simply an urban myth.

At four o'clock each day the opposing factions would gather on a hillside to throw clods of turf at each other and the Catholics would shout, 'Proddie dogs eat the frogs,' and we'd shout back, 'Catholic rats eat the cats,' and they retort, 'Naw we don't, this is Friday so we're having fish.' It never got any nastier than that, not initially anyway. We'd see the Catholic kids being taken to the chapel in what we assumed were wedding outfits. The wee boys in suits, and the wee girls in mini wedding dresses. We didn't know it was their Confirmation, we just thought they married young.

When I was nine I was sent to a social experiment called the Trondra Place Annexe. My new school Easthall was going to be completed in six months but before I was to attend it Glasgow Corporation's Education Department decided to conduct an experiment which entailed sending both Protestant and Catholic kids to the same school. I say school but the experiment was so half-hearted that it wasn't even a proper school. It was a block of six newly built closes that they'd neglected to partition off into bedrooms, kitchens, living rooms, etc, but had walled in to create classrooms. They also fenced it off with ten-foot-high mesh and I think it was on the second day that it was renamed the Gulag. Not by the pupils but by the teachers. It was a completely pointless exercise because the classes weren't mixed and the only time we did 'integrate' was at playtime. So there wasn't much of a lesson in religious harmony to be learned from Gulag schooling.

During my time there I only really learned one thing and it was in the playground, and it wasn't learned from a teacher, it was learned from listening to Catholic girls skipping ropes to the rhythm of the singing of: 'King Billy had a ten foot willie, took it to the woman next door, she thought it was snake, she hit it with a rake, now it's only three feet four.' There was a Protestant skipping rope reply to this, which began with: 'Hail, hail, the Pope's in jail . . .' but what the rest of it was I can't recall.

After the experiment was over I was sent to Easthall School and I actually took things in because at that point when I was asked what I wanted to be when I grew up I always said, without hesitation, 'A bin man.' Why? Well for a start they got to ride on the back of the bin lorries, which must have been quite exciting. My career choice was aimed slightly higher than a job with the Cleansing Department thanks to the influence of my teacher Mr McFarlane. He lectured that although we were the children of a working class background there was nothing wrong with the betterment of one's social standing and he gave us inspired speeches on great Scots who had risen from the ranks of the under privileged to become doctors, soldiers, politicians and inventors. Up until he told us we were under privileged we'd no idea we were, especially me because I thought, 'Under privileged? I cannae be, we've got chocolate biscuits in the hoose.'

Mr McFarlane would say, 'Name me one famous bin man.' Well there was one – Rakey Russell, the epitome of his profession, the ultimate midgie man. Rakey became a legend because of his ability to find riches amongst the rubbish, and he would share his soup from a flask with us on cold winter mornings and for that he was well liked. His back garden was like the yard in Steptoe and Sons as every treasure he found had a use and he could fix almost anything. A broken chair, a burst couch, he even found a use for old 78rpm records by melting them and moulding them into plant pots for his garden. Basically, what other people threw away he treated like the lost treasure of the Incas.

A NEW LIFE

Rakey was deemed well off because he had a car. His Ford Anglia was a sign of affluence to us, as car owners were few and far between in Easterhouse, so much so that the Easterhouse chapter of the Tufty Club Road Safety Campaign had zero members. The chances of being knocked down were less than zero, and to get knocked down by a car would have meant having to go really, really out of your way to position yourself in front of one. Rakey's car was funded by the money he made from the woollens he found on his route. Rakey got money for his discarded woollens, all we got for ours was a balloon from the ragman. Therefore Rakey was smart, we weren't. Rakey lived with his brother, a man simply known as 'The Knifeman'. Not because he went around stabbing people but because he went around the scheme with a whetstone on a wooden trolley he'd made for sharpening knives. He'd blow a bugle to indicate his presence and for sixpence he'd sharpen any knife on the whetstone that he operated with a foot pedal. He usually drew a decent-sized crowd of kids who gathered to watch the sparks and go 'ooooh'. He ended up in trouble with the police after they'd got a tip off that he was sharpening steel combs for gang members, who were trying to get around the laws regarding the carrying of offensive weapons by having the implement of a hair care regime sharpened into a 'steelie'.

Business was always brisk for the Knifeman as the company JML didn't exist in the sixties. Therefore, no one had their own knife sharpener, unlike today when for a mere £5.99 you can pop into Tesco, Asda, Focus or many other leading stores and buy a JML knife sharpener. I'm quoting the adverts here, which are always, 'New from JML, a thing that does stuff.' Sadly for the Knifeman, he wasn't very tall and stood about four foot eleven, and he looked even smaller compared to the big Easterhouse women. I'm talking big women who all had their hair in a beehive. To this day every time I see Big Kim from C4's *How Clean Is Your House* I think of the queue of big Easterhouse women waiting to have their knives sharpened by the Knifeman.

Mr McFarlane was a nice man, but he persisted with the downtrodden working class thing. He wrongly assumed that our parents never took us anywhere educational and this just wasn't true. Me, I practically lived in the Glasgow Museum and Art Gallery. To show us how right he always was and how wrong our parents always were he arranged a school trip to Glasgow Cathedral. We all boarded a bus and headed for the Cathedral. Now I don't know what route he thought the bus was taking but he must have decided we were on Duke Street because he pointed up a hill and said, 'There's Glasgow Cathedral up there.' The bus was actually on Alexandra Parade and he was pointing at some random church and I told him, 'No sir, Glasgow Cathedral is down there.' I knew exactly where it was because my Mother, thanks to various female problems, was in the Royal Infirmary more times than most of the staff. He wasn't pleased at all about being shown up by a mere member of the lower working classes who weren't supposed to know anything that he hadn't taught them.

As my mother was in and out of the Royal so much, it fell to me, as an eleven-year-old, to prepare the family dinner when she was in for one of her many operations. There were no worries in those pre-wrapping-kids-in-cotton-wool days about an eleven-year-old being left in charge of a chip pan. Although in retrospect there should have been because I put the chip pan on to prepare the dinner and thanks to a particularly interesting segment on *Blue Peter* about the new Churchill tank I completely forgot about it. When I eventually smelt the smoke I had the presence of mind to get my brother, who was six by this time, out onto the veranda along with the family budgie in his cage. My thinking being that budgies and small brothers are especially prone to the effects of smoke inhalation. This done, I went to deal with the fire and, not wanting to burn the kitchen down, I stupidly carried the burning chip pan through to the living room and put it in the fireplace. I was just in the middle of wetting a towel to extinguish the flames when my Dad burst through the door. He'd been coming along the road from work and saw my brother and the budgie on the veranda and whiffs of smoke coming out through the door. All was well though as I'd saved the house from burning down in a fire that was almost nearly about 10% my fault. The other 90% was surely the fault of parents who leave their eleven-year-old kid to fry chips. I didn't get much of a telling off because a) the house didn't burn down and b) I think my Dad did realise that perhaps I was indeed a bit too young to have that much responsibility thrust upon me.

When I told Mr MacFarlane what had happened he was incredulous, not at an eleven-year-old having the savoir faire to deal with a chip pan fire, but at an eleven-year-old being left alone in the house to cook dinner. To him it justified all the things he said about the people who lived in Easterhouse. But give him his due because he did devote almost a whole after-noon to fire prevention so that everyone else in the class would know how to put out a chip pan fire. At the beginning of the lesson he didn't say, 'In the extremely unlikely event of,' he said, 'In the extremely likely event.' I don't know if he was being sarcastic or he genuinely now thought everyone in his class made chips.

The headmaster at Easthall was a Mr McDonald who hailed from the Isle of Lewis. He was a Gael and most of the teachers at the school were Gaels too who he'd persuaded to join him. I think they all saw themselves at Gaelic Sidney Poitiers in their own personal *To Sir, with Love*. They wanted to bask in the warm glow of self-satisfaction they thought they'd get by teaching in a deprived area. Despite them all being Gaelic, they didn't teach us the language. I wish they had because I'd be driving around in a Ferrari thanks to an overpaid job at BBC Scotland or a seat on the board of the completely over-funded Gaelic language quango Bord Na Gaidhlig. In the sixties, the Gaelic language was considered quaint, today, though, being able to speak the language is a ticket for the Gaelic gravy train. I could learn the language now I suppose but you're not allowed to unless your name is Farquhar, you have a beard, an extensive collection of knitwear and live in the West End of Glasgow. And the rules for men are just as strict.

The language we were taught was French and we were taught through what Mr McDonald referred to as the medium of the electric television. Electric? That made us wonder what exactly powered the TVs on Lewis. Peat powered TVs? Who knows? It probably wasn't peat because it gives off the same heat as a damp piece of cardboard.

The school's electric television was, for the times, enormous. It was a giant, twenty-two-inch, black and white job encased in a wooden cabinet on long metal legs with wheels that was wheeled into the classroom by the headie. He didn't trust the jannie with his new piece of state-of-the-art, high-tech kit so he took the telly everywhere himself. He plugged it in, positioned it in front of the class and left Mr McFarlane to supervise the class learning French.

The problem with the French language programme was the presenter Madame Anne Slack and her puppets Clicko and Patapoof. Her surname alone was enough to produce sniggers, but every time she said the name Patapoof, that was it. Howls of derision filled the classroom. This led to Mr McFarlane running round the room smashing his belt off desks and threatening to belt us if we didn't calm down. His threats went unheeded because we were way past reason. Come on, Patapoof? It didn't end well as Madame Anne Slack's plea to repeat after me 'Je m'appelle Patapoof' was met with a united chorus of 'piss off'. The whole class got belted for that. My classmate Eddie Beattie got a double dose because he also shouted that Madame Anne Slack should 'show us yer tits'. We were eleven, what purpose would that serve? But he must have been taking the lessons in because he shouted, 'Montrer nous votre mamelles,' which, apart from probably at least four wrong tenses, is indeed almost perfect French for apprentice pervert Eddie's request.

Use of the belt was prevalent in those days and was used for every minor infringement of school rules, of which there were many. When the teacher was taking the register one morning, one of my classmates, who'd been watching the US cavalry sergeant taking roll call on the TV show *Boots and Saddles*, shouted 'yo', US cavalry style, instead of saying 'present' when his name was called out, and was belted for something that was really quite innocuous. Me, I was once given the belt for being in possession of an American Civil War card, which the school had banned due to the graphic nature. Looking back, the cards, which came in a pack of bubble gum, were pretty graphic and the particular card I was caught with showed Confederate soldiers impaled on large wooden stakes during an attack on a Union gun emplacement. I did give up collecting them after that and moved on to collecting Vietnam War cards. No Pannini footballer cards for us, we much preferred the gory depictions of war.

While the belt worked, getting lines did not strike the same fear into us. Plus, where was the glory in lines? After we'd been summoned to the headies office, the question asked was, 'How many did you get?'

'Nane, I got lines.'

'Lines, ya poof!'

The word poof wasn't used in any homophobic sense, it was just the general term used in every derogatory situation. A sort of utility word that covered every conceivable occasion. Even when the occasion made absolutely no sense, as in, 'What you daeing talking to burds . . . ya poof.' Yes, it was the Mr Kipling cake of abuse.

We all fancied the girls, but at ten the only way to show any affection was to steal their skipping ropes, their scrapbooks, which only contained fat cherubs, or punch them on the arm. The girls never understood our pre-pubescent chest beating and the recipient of our adoration would go and get their screaming banshee of a mother who'd threaten to 'tan oor arses fur us'. The mothers always appeared wearing curlers under a headscarf, slippers and a housecoat that flapped open to reveal tartan legs. That was the daytime look for an Easterhouse woman; it was their nighttime look too.

Relatives were used a lot in threats and we'd hear, 'I'm getting ma Mammie to you,' or, 'I'm getting ma Da to you,' and one threat I heard was: 'Ma brothers no all there by the way.' I think this was probably a certified medical statement on their kin's state of mind so it did pay to read between the lines. There was one particular mother who was never away from people's doors lodging complaints about the treatment of her son by the householder's offspring. She was known as Effie. Her real name was Mary but they called her Effie because she swore a lot.

Mind you, half the people in Easterhouse had some sort of mental issue. Our school maddie was a big guy called Hatchford who was indeed nicknamed Maddie and never was a nickname better earned. The best that could be said of Hatchford was: 'See him, he's no right.' He'd take scary brainstorms at the slightest provocation and Maddie-baiting became a pastime in our gang.

Not gang in the 'violent running around with open razors' sense, more along the lines of a *Famous Five*-ish sort of gang. The rules were simple. You had to stand and repeat loudly over and over that Maddie was 'it'. Although for some reason we pronounced it 'het'. Maddie took being 'it' as some sort of personal slight and would chase the person heckling him to the ends of the earth, through walls, under oceans, across international datelines, with the single purpose of relieving himself of being 'it'. My mate Eddie and I were in the back court one day and we saw Maddie grunting by, on the way no doubt to pull the legs off a daddy longlegs or a dog or somebody who'd crossed him. And being a bit bored we started chanting, 'Maddie's it, Maddie's it.' He stopped and looked at us. Obviously he had heard the noise but it was taking time to get through his ears and along the ear canal, past the thoughts of evil and into his brain. Once he twigged, he lumbered into action and started towards us with a menacing look on his face. We read the signals and got off our marks. He chased us from the back court, through the park, across playing fields, over hills and dales and in the general direction of Edinburgh. His pace never changed, it was a slow steady 'youse are pure dead' accompanied by the solid thump of his feet, which seemed to be keeping in time with our beating hearts.

The pursuit had been going on for half an hour and our legs were starting to tire but we daren't stop. Eventually we reached a metal railing, which wasn't high but I just couldn't get over it. Eddie managed it with one bound and ran off until he was a speck in the distance. Me, I just collapsed on the wrong side of it and Maddie stood over me blotting out the sun. I closed my eyes and waited for the inevitable kicking, but he just tigged me and walked off. I thought, 'Well he's obviously even more mental than we thought he was.' Twenty minutes later Eddie, stricken by guilt over abandoning me, came back to mop up the blood, but there seemed a lot more mileage in telling him that I'd seen Maddie off than admitting that Maddie just tigged me and left. So I went with the former story, which became more exaggerated every time I told it, and by about the twentieth telling it had become so exaggerated that people stopped believing that I'd stood up to Maddie because by this time I had him armed with a bazooka.

Many years later, Maddie proved the farsighted nickname we'd given him correct by ringing someone's bell and shooting the man through the letterbox when he was on the way to answer the door. The man survived and Maddie ended up in Barlinnie where the nickname Maddie was replaced by 'The Postman'.

There was one other slightly lesser Maddie at the school whose name was Grant. The G was silent because rant he did. He ranted about absolutely everything. The teachers, the school dinner menu and, as he was pretty intelligent, like way beyond his years, he ranted about America's policy of napalming Vietnam. It was the late-ish sixties and the hippy peace and love thing was just kicking in and both his parents could, I suppose, have been called hippies. What I didn't get was that, despite being eleven by this time, he wore a combat jacket and an American flag t-shirt to school, which begged the question, 'If you hate America so much, explain the t-shirt.' He was forever being sent home for breaching school uniform guidelines but neither he nor his parents cared.

He was such a child of hippy parents that he had a poster of Che Guevara on his bedroom wall. I had no idea who Che Guevara was and I thought the poster was of the bass player from the band Dave Dee, Dozy, Beaky, Mick and Tich. gRant also had quite long hair when no one else at the school did. No boy at the school had anything even near approaching long hair. This was because there was only one barber in Easterhouse and he operated from a converted single decker bus. No matter the style you asked for, Barber Sam gave you a short back and sides, and if that wasn't bad enough, he would put what he called 'cream' on it. Today it would be called styling mousse, not that it really was because this cream, whatever it was, was more like a jelly cement. When this stuff solidified on your head you could only comb your hair with the aid of a hammer and chisel.

Sam had a creepy limp, due to a wound he received in the Korean War. The reason I thought it was a creepy limp was because it wasn't your normal limp, it was the same dragging limp a Mummy has when it's limping after someone to extract revenge for disturbing his 3,000-year-old tomb. Sadly for Sam, he short-back-and-sided and creamed the wrong person and as a result, his bus was blown up by someone sticking a banger in its petrol tank. That boom led to a new era in tonsorial freedom in Easterhouse and slowly but surely our hair got longer and longer, not as long as gRant's, though, because, if you'll excuse the pun, he had a head start on us.

Everyone's long hair looked good from a distance but from close up it was frizzy, dull and lifeless because hair conditioners didn't exist until the early seventies. I'm saying frizzy but it wasn't always just frizzy as over-combing had left many people looking as though they had a full head of pubic hair. The only hair products available were shampoo and Brylcreem, although it was said if you washed your hair with beer or eggs they gave it a lovely shine.

Actually there was another hair product available called Derbac soap. It was a brown bar of medicated soap used to fend off nits and head lice. If you were poor your hair was washed with this, but for the lucky ones whose family budget could stretch to it they had theirs washed with Vosene Medicated Shampoo. As they said in the famous Monty Python sketch it was luxury, bloody luxury. Vosene was quite strong stuff and it was easy to tell who was using it because if you passed their house on Sunday bath night you could hear screams of: 'My eyes, my eyes, I've gone blind.'

While we're still on the tales of hair, I met gRant quite recently and ironically he is now totally baldy. I'm assuming he is because it looked like the shaved baldy thing and no one shaves their head unless they are baldy and doing that 'I'm not baldy I like my head shaved' thing that baldy men can get away with nowadays. In other words, shaving your head is the Bobby Charlton comb over for the new millennium. Head shaving hadn't become the thing to do in the sixties, seventies or even the eighties, and baldy blokes had the small band of hair that ran around their heads. Some even tried to compensate by letting what they had grow long, but it just looked ridiculous and a bit sad.

When the head shaving thing started it really infuriated my mate Jimmy the Saint because he reckoned that women never go out with baldy men, which meant there were more women for the follicley blessed. Now that there are all these shaven-headed blokes going about confusing women it lessened the field for him and, taking the moral high ground, he also thought it was incredibly dishonest of them.

gRant informed me, upon our meeting, that he was a committed socialist. Why he had to tell me he was a committed socialist as opposed to just a socialist wasn't exactly clear. But I had figured out his socialist leanings because he was still doing the Che Guevara thing and was wearing a Che Guevara t-shirt. Given that Guevara was a psychopathic murder, anything Guevara-related is an odd thing for a socialist to wear. Personally, I don't think anyone should wear a Che Guevara t-shirt unless they are trying to be ironic. He was also still ranting but oddly, despite his committed socialism, his rants weren't political. His ire now, and I have no reason why, was directed towards the TV chef James Martin. gRant ranted over Martin having a motoring column in the *Mail On Sunday*'s magazine *Live* and although I can't remember the rant verbatim, the gist of it was, 'Aye he's got a motoring column wae him stauning there in front of fancy motors wae a smug look on his face, he's a fucking chef, what does a fucking chef know about motors, I mean if ye wanted to know about food man, ye wouldnae go tae a fucking mechanic would ye?' He has a point, but what the point of that point is . . .

Anyway, what is a committed socialist doing reading the *Mail on Sunday*? If there's a newspaper that's the polar opposite of socialism it's the *Mail on Sunday*. Plus, what is the point of socialism? Socialism never works because people like owning stuff. Apart from that, socialist parties always spectacularly implode in on themselves, but on the upside, their implosion is a hilarious thing to watch.

I have two rules that I live by and they've served me well in life. The first is, never get a credit card from a woman at the airport who approaches you with credit card application forms attached to a clipboard, and the second is, never trust anyone who calls you brother. That, of course, doesn't apply if it's your brother who is calling you brother. If the person calling you brother isn't a very close blood relative the chance is that he is a fud with an over-inflated opinion of himself. When I say 'the chance is', I mean the chance is 100%.

3

GOODBYE TO SHORT TROUSERS

My last few months at primary school were spent preparing for my secondary school education. At secondary, classes were allocated by the intelligence levels graded at primary. Throughout primary I still managed to be either First or Second in the class and I had by now quite a library of slightly racist school prize books to prove it so I was assured a place in the A class. I'm pretty sure that's not how things are done today but in 1969, Glasgow Corporation Education Department's policy was very much Aldous Huxley's *Brave New World*. This meant that even at the age of twelve you'd been graded and would be educated according to your ability. If you were an Alpha you'd be educated properly and if you'd been graded an Epsilon you'd be stuck in a class, handed a crayon and told not to eat it. Basically they'd already decided whether or not to give up on you. They neglected to even contemplate that some pupils might be late starters, much preferring not to waste resources on good-for-nothings who'll come to nothing.

I could have bypassed all the pigeonholing because I had been offered a scholarship to attend the posh Allan Glen's School but although my parents wanted me to go, I really didn't fancy being, well, fancy. They'd have taught me to talk with marbles in my mouth and anyone who talked with marbles in their mouth in Easterhouse was asking to end up with a mouth full of marbles. And I mean that in the literal sense. Another reason I didn't want to go was because I had heard that they made their pupils wear school shorts up until two years after they'd left.

And they played rugby, and not being an Edinburgh solicitor or a Borders farmer, I had absolutely no interest in a game the rules of which state quite categorically that it's perfectly legal to try to yank someone's privates off during a scrum. The main reason, however, that wild horses couldn't have dragged me to Allan Glen's was because it was boys only, and the poor 'boys' who ended up there must have had the pishiest puberty ever. Perhaps, though, with no girls around, you don't get any puberty. Probably explains all the private pulling during scrums.

My scholarship refusal meant my big school wasn't going to be Allan Glen's, it was going to be Westwood and as the summer approached, we were taken on a pre-attendance tour. The only subtle difference I could see between a primary classroom and a secondary classroom was that the desks were bigger. The much less subtle difference was that teachers looked like proper teachers. Not that I'm saying that primary teachers aren't proper teachers, they are, but they are proper teachers whose demeanour is very much like a kids' TV show presenter – whatever happened they could say, 'I know a song about that.' The secondary teacher's demeanour was more 'step out of line and I'll thrash you to within an inch of your life'. And of course, thrashing was allowed as a method of class control back then.

After a tour of the school, we were taken to the assembly hall where the headmaster, Mr Waddell, addressed us. All I remember from his address was his assurance that he'd do his best to crack down on the traditional first day of secondary initiation doing inflicted on new starts by older pupils. We weren't at Westwood yet but we were being informed in no uncertain terms that when we got there, our wellbeing and survival depended on the success or failure of his crackdown.

I left Easthall in the summer of '69, the summer of love, which left me two months of wondering if the love would extend to my first day of secondary. It would be just the ironic thing to be beaten up by a bigger boy wearing love beads. As it was the summer of love, everyone was wearing love beads, which were so popular even the local newsagent sold them. I remember watching the gang fights that summer and thinking that the love beads weren't working. The gang violence that summer made absolutely no sense. On the TV news hippies in kaftans and flares were sticking flowers in the barrels of rifles, meanwhile, in Easterhouse, gangs in kaftans and flares were chasing each other around with machetes. Peace and love, man, right enough, eh? They liked the theory obviously, but just couldn't be arsed with the practice.

We did indeed spend the summer worrying. The 'we' was Eddie Beattie, Jacko, Wilco and myself. Eddie was philosophical about it and would often say, 'If they do us, they do us, so what?' This was fair enough but he was only so philosophical because he had a plan to avoid it by spitting on anyone who came anywhere near him. He had a gap in his front teeth and could impressively spit twenty yards. But spitting, that was it. He claimed that no one likes being spat on, which is of course true, but I pointed out to him that surely spitting, apart from being disgusting and unhygienic, would more than likely lead to a double kicking from whomever was spat on. Yes, good plan, but best to formulate a plan B, which we did. Plan B was to start crying and hope for mercy.

I did make the mistake of using the word 'whomever' when explaining that spitting could lead to a double kicking and the reply to my verbal faux pas was: 'Whomever? Who the fuck do you think you are, Lord Snooty, ya wanker?' Whomever, that's Allan Glen patter. The summer of '69 was the summer of Woodstock, the moon landing, Charles Manson and the aboli- tion of the death penalty in the UK. The abolition of the death penalty heralded the end of the swinging sixties, which was only called the swinging sixties because they still hung people back then. Although none of us were at Woodstock, obviously, the music of The Who, Jimi Hendrix and Crosby, Stills, Nash and Young could be heard on every street. This was because people had a penchant for opening their window and positioning their Dansette on the windowsill. This was them showing off how 'with it' they were. 'With it' was the phrase for 'trendy' back then. Seemed they thought 'listen to what I'm listening to' impressed people. Not that it really did because most passers by simply thought, 'What a fud.' Much the same way today as the driver with the car blasting out 100 decibels with the windows open is thought of as 'a total fud'.

The problem in '69 was the technology (and that's the first time a Dansette has ever been referred to as technology), as Dansette record players weren't that great and at full volume the casing rattled, so most of the time all you could hear was the rattle. Records also stuck a lot and many times you'd walk past a window and hear The Who singing, 'Talkin' bout . . . talkin' bout . . . talkin' bout . . .' This could only be rectified by either pushing the arm containing the needle along a bit to get to the 'my generation' bit or by balancing a penny on the arm to dig the needle into the grooves. I'm talking about the old heavy penny that weighed a couple of pounds, as decimalisation was still two years away. The more blunt the needle on the record player became, the more pennies it required, and when you got to a foot high stack of pennies, which added up to £1.19.11d, it was really time to use that £1.19.11d to buy a new needle.

I was allowed to stay up late to watch the moon landing, an event that was supposed to change the world forever. One small step for man, one giant leap for mankind. The giant leap, it transpired, was only a giant leap in the frying pan and clothing industry thanks to the development of Teflon and Velcro. Although the moon landing did give Michael Jackson the excuse to moon walk, which he used to distract people from noticing that he was grabbing his own crotch. Unfortunately for him, his moon walking eventually wasn't enough of a distraction to stop people noticing that he was allegedly grabbing other people's crotches too.

In an attempt to capture the mood of the time, *Blue Peter* that very week showed how to make your own brilliant and very lifelike Apollo 11 using the obligatory squeezy bottles, sticky back plastic and other everyday items you can find lying about the house. Every household did have sticky back plastic in the kitchen because it was much cheaper to cover kitchen work surfaces in it than in formica. These were the days of John Noakes, Peter Purves and Valerie Singleton, whom Wilco thought it hilarious to call John Nooky, Peter Pooves and Valerie Singletit. Mind you, he did that a lot, as there was another kids programme on then called *Junior Showtime*, which starred Glyn Poole, Miss Marjorie and Bobby Bennett, whom he renamed Glyn Poof, Miss Marjalezzie and Bobby Bent. What Freud would have made of his sexual renaming is anyone's guess.

I did make the *Blue Peter* Apollo 11, but it wasn't brilliant or lifelike. It was pish, and even more pish compared to the Airfix Apollo 11 Wilco built. So I never trusted *Blue Peter* and their lies ever again; lies such as, 'Your Mummy will be really impressed with this paper hankie box/holder thing you can make for her as a Christmas present,' and, 'If you collect used milk bottle tops and send them to us we can save the whole of Africa from starvation.' I was never convinced that all the money they made from used milk bottle tops reached Africa. I was always thinking, 'Here, how come the Blue Peter cat Jason can afford ANOTHER new collar?' and, 'New floral shirt Peter, won the pools have you?' I mean, how can you have faith in people who insist that the best Father's Day present is a homemade pipe holder? No one smokes a pipe. Certainly in Easterhouse no one did, probably because they'd have got their head kicked in for being a diddy. When *Blue Peter* weren't collecting for the poor and starving in Africa, their other biggie was Guide Dogs for the Blind. My school got involved in that one and put a bin inside the entrance for pupils to deposit their donated milk bottle tops. There was a sign above the bin that read 'Guide Dogs For the Blind' that someone had changed to 'Blind Dogs For the Guides'. I thought that was clever and hilarious, I still do.

As for the Manson Family, they certainly put the families in Easterhouse that we thought were bad into some sort of perspective. There was a family called Manson in Aberdalgie Place and they did have a son called Charles. But after the Manson Family's killing spree, he insisted on being called Chick. He must have been worried that people might confuse him with his namesake and cross the road to avoid him just in case he cult-murdered them. Thinking back, people crossed the road to avoid him anyway because he was a bit of a bam. Not that they had to bother, as he was more of a danger to himself than anyone else; in one gang fight, he somehow managed to chop two of his own fingers off with a machete.

The big summer movie in 1969 was *The Love Bug*, the tale of a Volkswagen Beetle called Herbie that had a mind of its own. Disney neglected to mention that the Volkswagen Beetle was originally designed by Ferdinand Porsche for Hitler and his Third Reich as a family run-around. Not so much *Herbie Goes To Monte Carlo* as *Herbie Annexes Sudetenland*.

In the week before I was to go to Westwood, my mother took me into Glasgow to buy me a new blazer and school tie. I explained that it was a waste of money because out of the 800 pupils who attended the school, I would be the only pupil there in a school blazer. Why single me out? Why don't you get a felt tip pen and write 'bully me' on my forehead? I also explained that it's only called a blazer because if I turn up at school on my first day in it someone will set it on fire, with me in it.

My protests fell on deaf ears, but on the subject of protests, the trip into Glasgow coincided with a protest in George Square against the Vietnam War. The protesters were students, students who'd watched the news and heard their American counterparts chanting, 'Hell no, we won't go, hell no, we won't go.' So that's what they were chanting too. It's seems to have escaped their intelligence that there was absolutely no reason why anyone would even ask them to go to 'Nam and this meant that their chant was utterly meaningless. But chant it they did.

You'd have thought they could have at least come up with their own chant, perhaps along the lines of: 'Hell no, we won't go, even though no one's asked us to, and it's highly unlikely they ever will.' So students haven't changed, still protesting and still trying to buy a bag of chips with a cheque.

It is amazing though how some things stick in your head forever. I remember another trip when I was dragged unwillingly around town shopping by mother and we came across two women who'd set up a trestle table in Argyle Street and on the table was a knitting needle, a metal coat hanger, a bottle of gin and a tin of Colman's powdered mustard. They were pro-abortionists calling for the legalisation and easy availability of the procedure because women were dying either at the hands of back street abortionists or from complications from self-inflicted abortions using what was laid out on the table. To this day I can still see that table quite clearly. That childhood vision has stayed with me for over forty years.

4

DANGER, DANGER, DANGER

Back to the first-day beating. I often wondered where this ritual came from, not that I had to wonder much as this school ritual came from where all school rituals came, public school. Thankfully by the time the ritual had filtered down from public school to normal schools it had gone from being rogered by a Peer of the Realm's son to simply getting a hiding from a ned.

The day duly arrived and we approached the school gates. It was like High Noon, except that it was nine o'clock. We were all wearing our school ties with very loose knots in a cocky men-of-the-world kind of a way, hoping that the reception committee would think that our act of sartorial rebellion would show them that we shared their maverick spirit of breaking school rules. The rule we were breaking was the strict dress code and the rule they were breaking was the much less strict not beating the crap out of a first year. There were about forty hardened pupils waiting, mostly third years with a few second years gathered on the fringes to sadistically enjoy the re-enactment of what they had gone through 365 days before. There wasn't a teacher in sight and then I saw the Janitor, who bore a striking resemblance to Sergeant Schultz in the TV programme *Hogan's Heroes*, disappearing round a corner with a brush. Schultz's catchphrase in the show was: 'I know nothing.' So was this guy's, either that or he genuinely did have a brushing up some broken glass emergency out of view of the school gates.

Eddie turned to us and said, 'Just do what I do.' The reply he got was: 'So we've to shit ourselves too then?' He looked at us and said, 'Look, it's under control.' They gathered round us and in the best tradition of the military, we formed a British Square, the same sort of British Square that had worked so well at Waterloo. Then again, Wellington's troops, or scum of the earth as he called them, were only facing Marshall Ney's cavalry, we were facing a foe much worse, we were facing the mentals.

The boots and fists came flying. I don't think the intent was entirely malicious, more of a case of 'well someone has to keep traditions alive'. We were saved when Eddie pulled an air pistol out of his haversack and shouted, 'Right ya bastards, fuck off.' They did all back down except for one of the second years who no doubt had suffered the year before and was determined to ensure that we were going to endure what he'd had to. He started shouting something about first years not ruling the roost and his words were starting to look as though they were shaming the mentals into action . . . until Eddie shot him in the thigh with a dart. This should have been the perfect time for them to rush us because the particular air pistol Eddie was waving about takes about forty-five minutes to reload because you have to apply two tons of pressure to get the firing chamber back into the barrel. But that didn't seem to have occurred to them and that was it, it was over, and of course, the moment it was over was when the teachers turned up.

'Break it up,' they shouted, which we would have done if there had been anything to break up. The bell rang and all the new starts were ushered into the assembly hall where we were allocated our class numbers. The curriculum was explained to us, we were to have different teachers for every subject and we were given schedules. French, Biology, Geography, Chemistry, Maths and so on, and our first class at secondary, for the boys anyway, was a double period Technical Drawing. We were separated from the girls who went off to Domestic Science, which was basically cookery, sewing and other such very important home maker pursuits, such as lessons in ensuring that their man's tea would be ready and on the table waiting for him when he got home from work.

After about ten minutes wandering the corridors we found the techie drawing class, inhabited by a giant of a man called Mr McConnell. Six foot six inches of complete and utter bastard. He acted as though he hated us even though he'd never set eyes on us before, but I found out later he wasn't acting – he just hated everyone. He towered over us explaining the rules of engagement. Speak out of turn, the belt, scratching the desk with a compass, the belt, late for class by even a millisecond, the belt, defacing your jotter, the belt . . . defacing your jotter, the belt?

That warning came too late for Wilco and Eddie because on the front of the jotter there was a road safety warning that read: 'Danger, Danger, Danger, better a moment at the kerb than a month in hospital'. After being handed their jotters in assembly, Wilco and Eddie had written R's over the D's and their warning now said Rangers, Rangers, Rangers. McConnell wandered round the class checking everyone's kit like a martinet and picked both of them from the ranks and paraded them in front of the class. Explanations that they didn't know they weren't allowed to vandalise their jotters because they were new were useless and he produced a belt from under his jacket. He wore it over his shoulder under his jacket and this thing could stand practically upright. We'd never seen a belt like it, as primary teachers' were quite flimsy fluffy things that gave your hands a nice warm feeling, the same nice warm feeling you could get from putting on gloves that have been on the radiator. His, though, meant business. He gave Wilco and Eddie two strokes each and the sting echoed round the room and the windows vibrated. Everyone in the class flinched with each stroke, except for Eddie who took the punishment with great fortitude. Not Wilco, he just blubbed.

There wasn't a mark on any of McConnell's desks or rubbers or rulers or anything after that. His classroom was pristine because he explained that every time we entered his class we had to check for any damage to school property and report it immediately. This would allow him to identify the culprit from the seat's previous incumbent. If we didn't report it, the incumbent after us would and we would therefore be blamed. Quite a good system as it happened. Technical drawing was a subject that everyone excelled at because the basis of it was drawing straight lines on a bit of paper, and since the school provided you with a ruler to do so it was kind of difficult to cock it up.

After that double period, it was playtime and it was during playtime that we met a couple of kids called Winker and Jim who'd come from the other primary school in the area, Blairtummock. Winker told us that his brother had been at the school few years beforehand and had warned him about McConnell. So that playtime we learned that our first impression of McConnell being a psycho was correct and we also learned that Jim had a very unusual nickname. Central heating didn't exist in Easterhouse council homes and as the houses were cold and especially freezing in the winter, most families had an upright paraffin heater, about three feet tall and with a grill at the top to let out the heat. At bath times it was taken into the bathroom to take the chill out of leaving the bath. Unfortunately, Jim had come out of the bath and leant up to get something off the shelf of the bathroom cabinet and his willie made contact with the grill. This had taken the skin off his boyhood and left it with the grill marks you see on a sausage. Once it was noticed in the showers by a genius of nicknaming, Jim was forever after known as Rumpel'dforeskin. Forever after, but not happily ever after.

Winker, on the other hand, was known as Winker simply because his surname was Watson and there was a Winker Watson in *The Beano* or *The Dandy* or some other such DC Thomson comic. He was only eleven but his IQ was almost off the chart and he'd been moved to the big school a year early because he was too smart to waste his time at primary. We spent the first few weeks getting to know the teachers, i.e. which ones we could wind up and which ones we couldn't. The easiest to wind up was Mr McLellan or Nutty as has was nicknamed. Nicknaming was big in those days, obviously, and the Nutty moniker came from his quick temper and the speed he could run down the class foaming at the mouth, hauling out miscreants. October and November were his least favourite months because that's when bangers were readily available in the shops and at the crucial parts of his chemistry experiments someone would let off a banger and he'd jump, drop his experiment and belt the whole class. This wasn't really much of a deterrent because he was right-handed and he had a shoulder problem, which meant he had to wield the belt with his left hand. Half the time he missed and half the time he made so little contact it felt as though he was hitting you with a woollen scarf. Having said that, chemistry was fun, fun in the sense of stealing strips of magnesium to throw into the urinals when someone was having a pee. If you remember your chemistry, magnesium reacts with water to produce a few seconds of a blinding white light, and many panicked pupils ended up sitting in classrooms with pish all down the front of their trousers. The comment to that was always, 'Moved up to the big boy pants a bit too early did we?'

In December that year we had a visit from a theatre group and we were taken down to the assembly hall where the chairs had been arranged in a huge semicircle. It soon became apparent why. It was audience participation theatre. Always the worst kind. At least this was free – I always get pissed off when you've paid for a theatre ticket and then you're expected to be part of the show you've paid for. This production, which was being toured round the schools, was about the Vietnam War. Still a big issue even though Easterhouse was about as far away as you could get from the Mekon Delta or the Perfume River. The show began when the 'actors' (I say actors, but you know . . .) ran on in American combat fatigues carrying plastic machine guns shouting, 'Body count, body count,' and dragging some of us off our seats and indicating that we were to lie on the floor kidding on we were dead. Once they were satisfied the body count was high enough they started shouting, 'Count the gooks, count the gooks.' Their words, not mine. What the message was still isn't clear but I'm sure it was an anti-war message of some sort. It was completely lost on us because it was delivered in subliminal performance art actor-y bullshit. If they simply said, 'War, what is it good for, absolutely nothing,' then we'd have got it. But they didn't, probably something to do with the Arts Council only funding theatre that people don't understand, a tradition that hasn't changed.

We left the auditorium with a pretty united feeling of 'what the fuck was that all about?' The actors had that smug actor thing about them too, as if they genuinely thought acting was a real and important job. To this day when I see most actors, not all I hasten to add, because I have to work with a lot of them, I think to myself, 'Away and get a real job.' This lot were particularly actor-y because after their 'show' a couple of us were told to help them load up their van and while doing so we heard them gushing all over each other on their performance. It was that exact moment when I decided that whichever professional career path I chose it definitely wouldn't be acting. Okay, I did marry a girl who spent three years at the Royal Scottish Academy of Music and Drama training to be an actress, but only because she'd never been in anything funded by the Arts Council.

Christmas was fast approaching and the corridors were festooned with crepe paper decorations and the practically remedial class of 1F's drawings of Santa. A feature of the end of term was the Christmas school dance and all through December we'd be dragged kicking and screaming into the assembly hall to be taught ballroom and Scottish country dancing. In 1969, it was *Come Dancing*, not the *Strictly Come Dancing* that it was relaunched as by the BBC. Somehow, and I have no idea how, the BBC have managed to make ballroom dancing 'marginally trendy' and I'm using the term 'marginally trendy' sarcastically here. In the less enlightened times, any boy who did ballroom dancing would get chased home every day by someone with a stick with a dollop of dog poo on the end of it. Sadly, that doesn't happen anymore and the males who do ballroom dancing today don't get stick-pooed for being tubes. This is despite them dancing with their noses so far in the air they look as though they are trying to smell shite on the back of their necks.

In 1969, no boy wanted to do ballroom dancing, nor Scottish country dancing for that matter, so we had to be forced. The boys would be lined up on one side of the hall and the girls on the side opposite. The teacher would say, 'Pick a partner,' and that would be met with the deafening silence of 'no chance'. It was only after many threats of the belt and then the use of the belt that we complied and shuffled across the hall and asked a girl to dance with a charming 'you'. We had to learn the lot, from the St Bernard Waltz to the Dashing White Sergeant and on to the Gay Gordons, which was, of course, long before Gordon came out of the closet. We never picked any girl we actually fancied because that would have led to embarrassing accusations of 'hey, you fancy her'. The fact that you took a beamer when you denied it with a 'naw I don't, I think she's a dog' just gave the game away that you did. The thinking, therefore, was that in picking a girl you didn't fancy, your denial would be beamerless and therefore true.

If you did have a girlfriend it wasn't called dating it was called 'going with' and it's estimated that 95% of schoolboy/schoolgirl relationships only ever began because a mate had broken the ice for them by informing one or the other that 'ma pal wants tae go wae you'. Not that you ever did really want to go with someone because it was all a bit embarrassing, what with the completely ignoring each other if your mates were with you, except for the times the ignoring didn't work because your mates thought it hilarious to push you into each other in the corridor. Dating at thirteen was pointless anyway in so many ways because we were an utterly different generation. In the five years I spent at Westwood, there was never a single instance of a confirmed teenage pregnancy. No one had sex; we weren't even sure what sex was.

That didn't stop the questions though, the main *après* date one being, 'Did you feel her?' and the reply was always the same, a quizzical, 'Feel her what?' There were rumours that a couple of fourth-year boys had in fact had 'a feel', but it was over the top of a Gloverall dufflecoat so I'm not sure that it really actually counted. If someone had said, 'She had some nipples on her,' it wouldn't have been nipples, it would have been the toggles on her dufflecoat. People did have a winch, in fact they winched so hard they ended up with frayed lips, and I'm pretty sure a lot of people passed out through lack of oxygen because they hadn't quite mastered breathing and kissing at the same time.

So, armed with dancing lessons, the night of the first-year school dance arrived. Although it was called the first-year school dance the more appropriate term should really have been the First-Year Shuffling-Self-Consciously-About-In-Front-Of-A-Girl Dance. We were all really shiny and stinking of Old Spice. Being pre- Denim, Brut and Hai Karate days, Old Spice was the only choice of aftershave there was. We hadn't had a shave but obviously we just wanted to smell nice. Well nice-ish, it was Old Spice after all. We'd also shared a whole can of lager that someone had stolen from his Dad's lager safe and we all thought we were steaming. After about half an hour, the dance was in full swing, as full as the swing was going to get anyway. Three or four couples were sharing the floor and Mr Murray, our registration and history teacher was walking amongst them separating anyone who was getting too close. An hour into it and we'd progressed to making eyes at the talent who were studiously ignoring us. Eventually, halfway through the night, the headmaster came on and gave the same sort of patronising speech we were to hear from him at every single school dance.

'Boys and girls, or should I say little ladies and little gentlemen, you are all looking splendid tonight, a credit to your parents, yes indeed. Now we have had the traditional music and now as a special treat we are to hear a couple of popular songs from the Westwood School group The Conspiracy. But before that I'd like you to give a big hand to Mr Murray and Miss McDowall who have given their time to chaperone tonight's event. Hip hip . . .'

All they got was two unenthusiastic handclaps, both coming from Murray and McDowall. 'Given their time', that was a joke. The minute the event was over they'd be in the back of his Triumph Herald in the school car park doing whatever it is grownups do to each other. It was the only reason they'd volunteered. I should add that it was generally agreed that Miss McDowall was the best looking teacher in the school and she must have been given just how many second year boys were crying themselves to sleep at night over her.

The Westwood School group came on, a sorry bunch of fourth-year terminal acne cases. You could see the pus seeping from fifty yards away. They subjected us to murderous renditions of the latest chart numbers. Their first was Creedence Clearwater Revival's 'Bad Moon Rising' followed by the Beatles 'Get Back'. I only knew what the songs were because they announced what they were before they played them. They had to because they were so bad we'd never have known otherwise. They were truly awful, and not just bad musically, the singer sounded like a bluebottle trapped in the curtains. Their set finished to no applause whatsoever, yet they still stood there waiting for it. Winker, who saw himself as an authority on music, summed them up best by shouting, 'What a load of absolute shite.' Now that did get applause.

Mr Murray made no effort to chastise Winker for swearing, more than likely because he agreed with him. Their drummer, who must have been fantasising that he was elsewhere with another group, got off his drum stool and with a flourish threw his drumsticks into the audience. No one made any attempt to catch them. Everyone stepped aside and they landed with a clatter on the dance floor. He walked off the stage to a well-deserved comment of 'ya fanny'.

Truth be told, the first-year school dance was terrible. Who in their right mind would force twelve- and thirteen-year-olds to dance to Jimmy Shand, the Joe Loss Orchestra or the Clyde Valley Stompers' 'There's A Moose Loose Aboot This Hoose'. We were young, not deaf. The next day was 24 December, the day we broke up for the holidays, and the day of the school's en masse annual pilgrimage to church for the Christmas service. The teachers looked upon this as the last battle of wits of the term as their job was to get 800 pupils to church and our job was to try to escape en route. They lined us up in the playground and we set off in a four-in-a-row line, which stretched about 400 yards with a teacher positioned at intervals of about twenty yards for the forced march. To onlookers we must have resembled a group of prisoners being escorted to a POW camp in Nazi Germany.

Most of us didn't fancy the prospect of spending two hours in a church and each year had its own escape committee. Our plan was to wait for someone to make a break for it and in the confusion we'd sneak away. We'd gone about 200 yards when two third years darted up a close. Murray spotted them and unwisely gave chase. This was our chance and Winker, Wilco, Rumpel'dforeskin and I ran up another close and onto the first floor landing. After five minutes, as we heard no footsteps in the close or the sound of a siren or barking Alsatian, we thought we were safe. So we came out of the close and walked straight into the headmaster who was bringing up the rear. Our name ended up in what he called his January Book, a book that contained a list of all the names of escapees he was to belt on the first day of the new term. We just hoped that it wasn't cold on the first day back and if it was, that he'd wait a couple of hours before summoning us for our punishment. At least then our hands might have warmed up because being belted with cold hands intensifies the pain tenfold.

Kids today might wonder why we accepted the belt. We did so because we thought that it was a lot better than the alternative in English schools, which was the cane, sometimes across the hands but more often than not across the buttocks. I mean, the buttocks, that's just barbaric. Not wanting to sound old and crusty but the belt did work as a method of discipline and I can't really envisage what my school would have been like without it. Probably ablaze. Actually it wouldn't have been ablaze since long after I left, the school had to be demolished because it was discovered that the material used to build the school was primarily asbestos. That certainly explained a lot, especially the many failures by arsonists to turn it into a pile of smouldering ashes.

During Christmas of 1969 the telly was the usual festive fare. There was the Christmas Morning Service, a Save the Children appeal from Barbara Mullen (I have no idea who Barbara Mullen is), A Very Merry Morning billed as 'Leslie Crowther joins the kids in Seacroft Children's Hospital Leeds'. In other words, the usual sentimental mince, but there was always two Christmas highlights in the shape of *The Morecambe and Wise Show* and the Christmas *Top of the Pops*. Good though Morecambe and Wise were, the highlight of every teenager's Christmas Day was *Top of the Pops* because it featured every number one that year. And 1969 was a particularly good year for music because Cliff Richard didn't have a number one hit single. Although to hear the great number ones we had to sit through some garbage in the process. For instance the great number ones that year were the Rolling Stones' 'Honky Tonk Woman', the Beatles' 'Get Back' and 'The Ballad of John and Yoko', Marvin Gaye's 'I Heard It Through The Grapevine', The Moves' 'Blackberry Way' and Fleetwood Mac's 'Albatross', but there was also the crap of Marmalade's 'Ob-La-Di, Ob-La-Da', The Archies' 'Sugar Sugar' and Rolf Harris's 'Two Little Boys'. And this was when Rolf wasn't considered ironic.

The BBC had a problem that year because Jane Birkin and

DANGER, DANGER, DANGER

Serge Gainsbourg had reached number one with 'Je t'aime . . . Moi Non Plus', which the Beeb had banned because they thought it was full of disgusting, dirty sex noise from a filthy, manky jezebel. They handled the controversy by completely ignoring that it had topped charts. In the sixties, seventies and eighties, achieving a number one hit single was a big deal but then the nineties came along and the rules changed – after which to reach number one, a record had to only sell something like seven copies. Look, when Michelle McManus has a number one single you know the music industry has a serious problem with credibility. A new number one each week meant far too many number ones and that in turn meant that the Christmas *Top of the Pops* would have to start on December 10 and run through until February to fit them all in. To hear your favourite group when you wanted, you actually had to buy the record because there was no illegal downloading. Admittedly some people did have cassette tape recorders and could tape the song off the radio by positioning a small microphone in front of the speaker but the quality was atrocious and the overall sound wasn't helped by the sound of your mother hovering in the background and the voice of the sound engineer saying, 'Aw come on Maw I'm trying to record this.'

Mothers always hoovered at the most inopportune times, i.e. when you were trying to record a song off the radio, or in front of the telly at the exact same time a goal is scored when you were watching the football. Generally speaking, we didn't actually watch TV that much because there wasn't that much to watch. What there was mostly seemed to come from Europe and was dubbed. I did like *The Flashing Blade*, the adventures of the Chevalier de Recci who every week managed to outdo his arch-rival Cardinal Richelieu. It also had a catchy theme tune called 'Fight' by The Musketeers. Being pedantic, the Chevalier de Recci didn't really have a blade as such; he had a rapier, which isn't really a proper sword, it's just a long, thin, pointy, sharp thing. Having said that, I don't think calling the programme *The Flashing Long, Thin, Pointy, Sharp Thing* would have enticed that many viewers.

Another dubbed favourite was *The Adventures of Robinson Crusoe* starring Robert Hoffman, which also had a catchy theme. This leads me to believe that they came up with a catchy tune first, then wrote a TV series based on it. There was also *The White Horses, Belle and Sebastian* and *The Singing Ringing Tree*, which scared the crap out everyone because it had an evil dwarf and a weird talking bear who was actually some sort of Prince thing. On the home-grown telly front there was *Follyfoot*, which was pants. It featured Gillian Blake, who had the worst feather cut in the history of terrible feather cuts, as Dora Maddocks and she was constantly worried about people killing horses. Every script started the same way with her in tears telling her co-star Steve, 'Oh Steve they are going to kill a horse, we must save it.' Which they did, roll the credits.

There was, of course, *Captain Pugwash* and *The Saga of Noggin the Nog*. *Noggin the Nogg* was drawn in dark eerie silhouettes, the exact same dark eerie silhouettes you see when you're coming down from an LSD trip. I only know this because someone, who obviously wasn't me, tried acid once or twice or twenty-three times and told me it was.

Glen Michael's Cartoon Cavalcade was unmissable, not so much for Glen, his lamp Paladin or his dog Rusty or Rudy (one dog died and was replaced with the other but I can't remember in which order) but for the cartoons. I particularly hated Sundays when it came to TV, especially in the winter, because it was designed to suck the life out of you, leaving you with barely the will to live. It got dark at four and you'd have had your tea and be stuck on the couch while your parents watched *Songs of Praise* or the even more hymmie singing *Stars on Sunday* with Jess Yates, who it later transpired wasn't Paula Yates's Dad at all. It was Hughie Green. The bible-bashing was followed by *The Black and White Minstrel Show* and that was just depressing, with people blacked-up and singing hits from the sixties. The 1860s.

DANGER, DANGER, DANGER

It was like a racist *White Heather Club. The White Heather Club?* It was on weekly and it was like having fifty-two New Year's Eves annually. The heuchter teuchter thing dominated the TV and when you're a teenager, you're sitting there thinking, 'Give me a fucking break.'

If it wasn't BBC Scotland's *White Heather Club* we were being tortured with, we were waterboarded with STV's *Thingummyjig* with Jack McLaughlin, otherwise known to himself as the Laird O' Coocaddens. His catchphrase was 'shoogle your wallies', although my mother used to shout to my Dad if he was in another room to 'come on through Alex and waggle your willies'. Mind you, my mother was always getting things wrong because many years later the TV newsreader appeared on *Stars In Their Eyes* singing 'Fever'. My mother told me, 'I saw your pal Kirsty Young on the telly and she was singing, "You Give Me Beaver".' No, Mum, she wasn't.

It was around this time that I thought my Dad was having an affair because when you are thirteen or so you take things quite literally. Not that I thought my Dad was having an affair with just anyone. I thought he was having an affair with Kathy Kirby, a popular singing star of the day. And why did I think my Dad was having an affair? Because every time Kathy appeared on a programme my mother would say, 'Look, Alex, your girl-friend's on the telly.'

The Scottish soap back then was STV's *Garnock Way*, of which I don't remember much except for the actor John Stahl's police-man character. The sleeves on his uniform were miles too short, so much so that it looked as though his uniform was short sleeved. He only even seemed to have one line, which was, 'Will you no go out with me Mary Baxter?' We had a girl in our class called Mary Baxter and we wiled away many a double period of Maths by rolling up our sleeves and asking her out.

For me, though, the highlight of the televisual week was *Crime Desk* with Bill Knox. It was hilarious, although it wasn't meant to be. Bill would tell you about crimes and ask the public's help in solving them, and of course, as he said, 'Calls made to the police can be in confidence.' What was funny about *Crime Desk* were the crimes because the crimes always seemed to involve the theft of a JCB. According to Bill, that's all that was ever stolen in Scotland and they were always stolen by neds, and it was never actually very clear when the neds stole them because Bill would say, 'Between the hours of 5pm on Friday and 10.50am on the following Wednesday, neds broke into a builder's yard and stole a JCB.' JCBs are big yellow things, so how did the owners not notice it was missing? Surely the big yellow thing not being where the big yellow thing usually is was a bit of a giveaway.

Bill was the first person to use the word ned on television. When I say use it, I mean overused it, because *Crime Desk* had a ned count of about 160 every show. The only time I think *Crime Desk* wasn't about stolen JCBs was when Bill asked for the public's help in catching Bible John. I often wonder how that panned out for him and the police.

There was a lot more religious programming than we have today and every weeknight STV broadcast *Late Call*, which ended up brilliantly parodied by Rikki Fulton on *Scotch and Wry*. The gist of 90% of *Late Call* shows was that it was much better to be a Protestant than a Catholic because Protestantism is very low maintenance as it doesn't require you having to do anything. You don't even have to go to church, which is just as well because Scotland wouldn't really have that many Protestants if church attendance was a rigidly adhered to requirement.

5

LEADER OF THE PAK

The sixties were drawing to a close and I don't think anyone in Easterhouse was sad to see the back of them, mainly because it was the decade when the area became notorious throughout Europe for gang violence. The area of Easterhouse had been divided into sub-areas and each sub-area was the domain of a gang. I don't know how this had been achieved, probably by some sort of gang summit where the gang leaders sat down and negotiated with each other which turf was theirs. The gang ruling the roost in my area were the Skinheads and we were bordered by the Torran Toi, the Drummie and the Bar-L, who came from just across the Edinburgh Road in Barlanark. If ever a gang were aptly named it was the Bar-L because most of them ended up in Barlinnie Prison.

It wasn't really bordered as such, it was more like surrounded. Occasionally the West Rebels and the Pak, who hailed from slightly further away, ventured into hostile territory and it never ended well. On one lovely summer's evening my mates and I sat on a gable end wall watching a fight between the Skinheads and the Pak. This was the only entertainment available and it usually helped pass quite a pleasant evening watching the sabre rattling. What made this encounter unusual was that there actually was a fight because normally someone would shout, 'Come intae me,' and one gang would charge and the other gang would run away. Then the same thing would happen in reverse. But on this evening they completely mistimed their charging and both charged at the same time. I was surprised that the two 'leaders aff' didn't meet in the middle and say, 'Come on, we had a meeting, we discussed this, we charge first, you run away, then after that it's your turn.' The outcome of the lack of choreography was brutal, with the Pak ending up on the losing side. Most of them eventually managed to escape, albeit with various slash and machete wounds, but two didn't. The first ended up stabbed up the rectum a couple of times to shouts of, 'Let's see if the Royal can fucking stitch that,' and, 'You'll be shitting out Play-Doh shapes.'

Turns out he was the lucky Pak member because the other one was lying on his back with two Skinheads holding his legs apart, while the third was swinging a golf club and trying for at least a two under par with his testicles. Judging from the noises he was making, the experience was less than pleasant for him. I'd love to say that I had sympathy for him but I didn't. If you are going to run around in a gang waving sharp things about, you really have to expect the occasional serious assault on your man junk by a maniac with a five iron. I'm saying it was a five iron, but it could have been a sand wedge. I wasn't getting off the wall to have a closer look.

Why machetes were used frequently was never something that could be explained but where did they get them? It's not as if they should be widely available for purchase, as Scotland is hardly a country known for its dense jungle undergrowth. The next morning we found that someone had spray painted Skin-heads 7 Pak 0 on the gable end we'd been sitting on. What had once been a gable end was now a scoreboard. It was said at the time that the Pak only lost because their leader, or 'leader aff' as it was more commonly known, was on holiday and hadn't taken part. This was probably true because their leader aff – Babs – was enormous and terrifying, and more to the point, he was completely mental. I once saw him yank a metal clothes pole out of the ground and swing it about like a medieval staff. So how enormous was he? Put it this way, he played the big bass drum in the Orange Walk but because of his gargantuan stature it looked like he had a snare drum strapped to his chest. So the Pak taking on the Skinheads without Babs was the equivalent of German tank divisions taking on the Russian tank divisions in the Battle of Kursk without their tanks.

I don't know why his nickname was Babs, probably because having a girlie nickname allowed him to get into many, many more fights with people who pointed that out to him, or anyone who even just thought it because legend had it that Babs could read minds. When Babs got back from holiday, the first thing he did was to chib his No. 2 for taking the decision to fight the Skinheads without him, a decision that saw the Pak's street gang rankings fall behind the Drummie, which was bad for the Pak because the Drummie were a bunch of diddies. The second thing he did was to demand a rematch but the Skinheads, while they may have been short on hair, weren't short on intelligence and declined with excuses like, 'Sorry, I'm staying in to wash my scalp,' or, 'Sorry, we've suddenly become pacifists and we've renounced violence.'

By 1968, the gang warfare had reached such a level that Easterhouse was awash with TV crews reporting on the impact the situation was having on the vast majority of people who had absolutely nothing to do with gangs. Having a TV crew in Easterhouse was never something that ended well, especially for politicians when appearing on camera making platitudes. Every interview would start with the politician's face to camera with no one in the background, but five seconds into the interview the background would be filled with neds who'd suddenly appeared from nowhere to flick the Vs or make the wanker sign behind the politician's back.

It's a tradition that continues to this day with the latest victim being the then Justice Minister Cathy Jamieson. There she was spouting forth about all that the Scottish Parliament and the Scottish Labour party were doing for disaffected youth and all the time a disaffected youth in a shell suit was flicking the Vs behind her back. It became an iconic image that left me strangely very proud of where I'd come from.

In actual fact, all the social commentary was patronising and in the end, utterly meaningless because it was never backed up with action. That was until Frankie Vaughan came along. Frankie, or Mr Moonlight as he was known because that was his biggest hit, read about Easterhouse, saw it on the TV news and on the Pathe News at the cinema, and decided that he had to do something about it. He'd grown up in Liverpool, which had a gang problem too, but Liverpool had the Beatles now so the city was world famous for something positive. We didn't have the Beatles to take the bad look off it so Frankie thought we needed help.

So what gave Frankie Vaughan the right to get involved in what was basically absolutely none of his business? He'd winched Marilyn Monroe so that gave him the right. Winching one of the most beautiful women in the world not only gave him the right, it made him a legend amongst winchers. There were those who claimed he was only doing it for the publicity but that was just jealously on the part of people who were jealous that they hadn't got to winch Marilyn Monroe. Yes, there was much local bemusement, but bemusement is much better than hostility.

Frankie called for a weapons amnesty that was much publicised and Frankie and the press descended on Easterhouse. A metal bin was provided as the receptacle for the weapons, but it was just one bin. By local reckoning, Frankie was about ninety-nine bins short of what would have been needed should the gangs genuinely disarm. Many gang members did indeed turn up carrying an assortment of weapons, some dangerous, but mostly just odd bits and pieces they'd found en route to the photo opportunity. 'Aye the Frankie Boy man, this is ma chibbing brick, which naw, I didnae just find it, naw, naw, me and this brick have been in hunners a' gang battles man,' and another ned, 'And see this bottle, see whit he's just said, well ditto, big Frankie man.'

The gangs may not have properly disarmed but what

Frankie's interest did achieve was to focus public attention on the area's problems. Up until then every story had simply been full of tut-tutting and verbal disdain but now there were calls for something to actually be done about it. Frankie started the ball rolling by donating £3,500 – the proceeds of his concert at the Glasgow Pavilion. This shamed Glasgow Council into action and they said they'd donate double what Frankie made. The £10,500 raised was spent on what was called the Easterhouse Project, the result of which was a couple of Nissen Huts erected just off Lochend Road. This may have sounded like a great idea, but unless you lived in the immediate area it was pointless because the gang borders still existed and you'd still get your head kicked in if you didn't hail from within an 800-yard radius of the huts. The attitude of the gang who ran the area was, 'Naw, I think you'll find that Frankie built *us* these Nissen huts, no youse, so fuck off.'

An odd thing happened when Frankie was in Easterhouse. My pet hamster disappeared. I looked everywhere. I say every-where but really I just looked behind the fridge because that's the usual place where hamsters turn up, dead or otherwise. Hammie was nowhere to be found so I came to the conclusion that, as Hammie's disappearance coincided with Mr Vaughan's visit to Easterhouse, Frankie Vaughan ate my hamster. Well you do hear about showbiz people and their strange goings on with small rodents, don't you? The rumours about Richard Gere and the gerbil, for instance, that I won't go into because it's all a bit weird.

So Frankie left and everything returned to normal. When I say normal, I mean normal for Easterhouse. Now you may ask where the police were in all this. Usually nowhere to be seen. No, not usually, always nowhere to be seen. This wasn't helped by the fact that Easterhouse didn't get a police station until 1972. But on the odd occasion when someone bothered to phone the police station in the city to report a pitched battle, they'd turn on the police sirens so that they could be heard from miles away in

Baillieston. If their plan was to let everyone know they were coming and give the gangs time to run away, then their plan worked brilliantly. When they did arrive, slowly, being overtaken by milk floats and pedestrians, the battle was over and there was no one to arrest. In all the years I lived in Easterhouse, I never ever heard anyone shouting, 'Run, here's the polis.' I did hear, 'Right, there's the polis sirens, that gives us a couple of hours to wrap this fight up and stroll off at a very leisurely pace.'

The police inaction led to vigilantism. A group of grown men decided to take the law into their own hands and formed what they called the White Panthers. But they were just as crap as the police. They travelled around in a blue Bedford minibus, not accosting any gang members but accosting plenty of innocent passers-by. I know this because one night my mates and I were walking along the road doing nothing of any consequence when the van screeched to a halt beside us, the grown-up men jumped out and they dragged us all into the back of the bus. Nowadays I think that would be called an abduction and false imprisonment. They played the hard-men card and threatened us, which pissed us off no end because it was an injustice. None of us were gang members. We knew the gang members and they knew us but that was because we'd made them aware of us. Our thinking came from The Beach Boys' song 'I Get Around', which contains the line 'the bad guys know us so they leave us alone'. It seemed to work.

The more the White Panthers questioned us as to what we were up to, where we lived, etc, the more belligerent we became and that resulted in the fattest one losing his temper and slapping Eddie across the face. At that point they realised they'd gone too far as Eddie told them, 'I'll get you done for assault ya fat bastard.' They opened the bus doors and let us go and that was it, our only run in with the White Panthers. If they'd tackled the gangs they would maybe have done some good but they didn't because they were basically ineffectual cowards.

The only positive of living in a gang-controlled area was the protection it sort of afforded. The gangs had some kind of distorted honour, which made them see themselves as the local inhabitants' protectors. The Skinheads' main members were Alka, Virgo and Nervo. Nervo had a nervous tic (hence the name). Knowing who they were was always handy when you were stopped by a minor member of the gang. In the American West, the Apache handed out a tomahawk with feathers attached in such a way that it acted as a sign of safe passage. Any traveller passing through their territory simply had to show it to a war party and they'd remain unscathed. In Easter-house, a name was our Apache tomahawk. When stopped by a Skinhead war party, you simply had to say, 'Alka, I know him,' and that would be it. But you had to ensure that the ned you were attempting to appease came from the gang which included the person's name you were dropping. If you got it wrong, the only other hope you had was that you were a faster runner than the other guy.

Of course, it did get ridiculous when, for instance, the ned didn't take your word for it and demanded to know how you knew Alka. This left you explaining, 'Well, see, his sister, she's got a pal whose going out with a guy who lives in the next close to me whose cousin's mate's pal's brother lives in Halliburton Crescent, and that's how I know Alka.' Usually the confusion confused them.

Alka, it has to be said, was responsible for the only working telephone box in Easterhouse, which was situated on Ware Road. Every other one was vandalised, but the Ware Road box was in perfect working condition because this was the box that Alka used to phone his girlfriend in Shettleston and he let it be known that anyone who damaged the phone box would end up being damaged by him. That phone box stood out as a beacon of normality in a world gone destructive.

One of the gangs bordering Skinheadland was the Torran Toi. They deserve a mention because they were the scariest gang of all. They came from Torran Road, a road no one ever ventured along. Like not ever, because even on the sunniest day it seemed to be shrouded in an evil fog. Torran Road was like Easterhouse's Castle Dracula. You could see it in the distance but you didn't want to go anywhere near it. The thing was, though, that they had a reputation and no one knew why. They were never in any gang fights, so where this reputation that they were all 'dead good fighters' came from was a mystery and even more of a mystery was why Torran Road was viewed with such trepidation. But it was and staying with the movie theme to labour the point, Torran Road could have been an alternative urban setting for *Deliverance*. It was all the plunk of banjos and the pretty mouth squealing of pigs.

There's a great line in Rab C. Nesbitt when Rab is up north with Jamesie and he tells him not to annoy the locals because 'they'll take ye up the hills and shag ye and eat ye'. That's how everyone saw Torran Road. The Torran Toi instilled fear in everyone and even the Skinheads mentioned their name in hushed tones.

It transpired, as I was to find out much later, that their reputation was unearned and completely unfounded. I had a mate called Kenny Lochhead who lived in Trondra Place, which was directly opposite Torran Road. All that separated him from them was a river of tarmac thirty feet across called Wellhouse Road. Kenny had this ridiculous Beagle called Nicky that was off its head. We were walking him one evening and Kenny stupidly let Nicky off the leash and he shot straight across Wellhouse Road, straight in the direction of Torran Road and straight in the direction of a group of the Torran Toi. Kenny ran after him shouting for me to go with him. I don't remember my exact words but I'm sure they were along the lines of, 'Aye, watch me, that's the Torran Toi.' So solo Kenny ran after Nicky yelling, 'Come on.' Then the strangest thing happened. The Torran Toi thought he was running at them, shouting, 'Come on,' and they ran away. There were about six of them, one of him, and they ran away. After that I never looked at the Torran Toi or Torran Road in the same terrifying light ever again.

As a footnote, Kenny's crazy dog broke his veranda window and nosed the fridge door open and ate all the plastic fittings. Not the food, just the plastic fittings, and he also ate the phone. His parents had to get rid of Nicky and told Kenny they'd given him to a farmer who was using him as a gun dog. Kenny actually believed that. He probably still does. Me, I always thought farmer was euphemism for vet and gun dog was a euphemism for put to sleep. So Kenny, if you happen to be reading this, your mother and father murdered your dog. Regardless of all the everyday violence, 99% of it was directed at opposing gang members and despite what people say about Easterhouse in that era, if you weren't involved in a gang, life was much the same as it was in most parts of Glasgow. No one lived in fear. Yes, there might have been short bursts of it, but in general it was as safe an environment as any for the civilians.

6

INTO THE SEVENTIES

So the seventies began. The decade when it was a very bad idea for rock stars to have names that started with the letter J. Jimi Hendrix, Jim Morrison and Janis Joplin all died from drug overdoses. The result of which was if you were a rock star whose name starts with the letter J, it's best not to bother making any long-term plans. For me it was back to Westwood, the school that wouldn't burn.

There was talk of a ban on the belt because some bleeding heart liberals, a teacher's words, not mine, were claiming that it was a barbaric practice. But the ban was years off and it was lucrative business as usual for the teachers' supplies company who provided them. I often wondered if the teachers were issued with a belt by the Education Department or if they bought their own. Perhaps the day they graduated as teachers they were issued with a belt and told, 'There you go, there's your Glasgow Education Department belt, swing it with pride and try not to hit yourself in the face with it.'

As it was all just talk about a ban on the belt, the headmaster announced over the tannoy who was to pay him a visit to be punished for doing a runner from the church service. I think that probably took up most of his first week back because it was a long, long list of names. His second week back was taken up with belting pupils who'd misbehaved at the service, and that was a long list too. In their defence, the church service was performed, if that's the right word, by the Reverend John Cook. He was a lovely man but through no fault of his own he was very partially deaf and this led to him singing slightly out of time with everyone else. Some people found this hilarious and those who couldn't hide their hilarity ended up on the headies list.

The Reverend Cook loved *Jesus Christ Superstar* and for a while the sermons he did when he visited the school weren't actually sermons at all, they were him playing *Jesus Christ Superstar* at the fullest volume the school's sound system could manage. Being so very partially deaf, this helped him hear it, albeit slightly, while everyone else in the assembly hall was lying writhing on the ground with blood pouring out of their ears.

Those who didn't find the Reverend Cook's out of time singing hilarious ended up on the list for finding the Reverend Cook's assistant absolutely hysterical. I can't remember his name but everyone called him Jesus because he was a trendy hippy minister with long hair and a beard and he looked like Jesus. He also wore a big wooden cross so large that if Jesus had been about a foot shorter he could have been nailed to it. But that wasn't what made people laugh, it was the fact that he called everyone 'man' and would punctuate his sermons with it. I'm sorry but there was something genuinely funny in hearing from him that the Good Lord was 'cool and groovy, man'. In the telling of the parable about Jesus changing the water into wine at the wedding in Cana he said, 'Jesus's mother said they have no more wine, and Jesus replied, what a downer, man.' I've looked in the Bible and nowhere does it say that Jesus ever said, 'What a downer, man.'

The main hilarity came when he played his acoustic guitar. I mean the guy was a walking cliché. The reason everyone laughed was because he just wasn't very good at it and when he was singing he had to stop singing every few seconds to change the chord. He was simply awful, as were his songs because they were always 'Michael Row The Boat Ashore' and 'Kum By Ya'. Someone can't play the guitar Lord, Kum By Ya, but that's not stopping him Lord, Kum By Ya. He never ever said goodbye when he was leaving; he always pointed and said, 'Remember, Jesus loves you,' and the reply he always got was, 'Yes, I know, and he wants me as a sunbeam.'

After the fortnight of the headmaster bringing his beltings up to date, he returned to his headmasterly duties and the spring term began in earnest. It was my birthday in February and having a birthday was a dangerous undertaking. No one admitted having a birthday because of the dumps. As I was turning thirteen this would mean that, according to some birthday by-law, each of my fellow pupils had to celebrate the thirteenth anniversary of the day of my birth by punching me fourteen times on the back. One for every year I'd managed to stay alive and one for luck. Although the one for luck was less of a rule and more of a guideline because they could punch you just for luck as many times as they wanted. I'm positive that people who suffer from back problems in later life have the dumps to thank for it because having your spine malkied with brutal force every year must surely leave some sort of long-term damage. On this occasion, I actually was lucky because no one knew it was my birthday and I escaped unscathed. My mates did know that my birthday was in February but they didn't know the exact date.

For my birthday that year my parents had got me a pair of Levi's, the ones you had to buy two sizes too big and sit in the bath in them until they shrunk to your size. The first time I wore them I was told, 'New denims by the way, you'd better have no got them for your birthday.' This would have meant my birthday had passed and I'd kept it to myself. Which I had. No one called them jeans back them, we called them denims. I have no idea why, other than Easterhouse had a lot of girls called Jean and this might have led to copyright problems.

I didn't know it at the time but my birthday jeans/denims led directly to me eye-witnessing events that eventually led to a murder. Two new families had moved into Wardie Road, one in the close to the left of me and one two closes to the right of me. I don't remember their names but the one to the left included the father who was as staunch an Orangeman as you could get and the one to the right included the father who was the Orangeman's mate and drove private coaches. Come the July marching season, the Orangeman who was in the Orange Walk (which, thinking back, seemed to have had a lot of members) would hang a large Red Hand of Ulster flag from his veranda. The flag in itself was bad enough but he also played 'The Sash' and 'No Surrender' at full blast through the open veranda door. Obviously a lovely, rational, tolerant chap.

There was one Catholic family in his close, the McLachlans, one of whom, Peter, was my pal. The Orangeman was the neighbour from hell, not just for the Catholics but for everyone because the Protestant/Catholic thing was never a local issue. The Protestants probably had more disdain for him because he was a total embarrassment to their faith. No one complained to him, though, as he was one of those people who you couldn't complain to because if you did, you'd end up on his 'list'. He did disappear to Belfast for two weeks and as it was right bang smack in the middle of the Troubles, it was rumoured he was away fighting for the UVF. He returned with a stooky on his arm and it was said he'd been shot in the arm. The Belfast connection was further confirmed one afternoon when Peter and I were accosted at the back of the close by a shifty looking bloke who asked us in an Irish accent if we knew where he was. Seems the Orangeman wasn't in and the Irishman was becoming impatient and wanted to know if we knew where he drank so that he could go and 'buy him a drink'. When the Irishman said 'buy him a drink' it was laced with menace. So much menace that Peter and I put two and two together and came up with IRA. We didn't know where the Orangeman drank so the Irishman left and we thought no more about it.

Now back to the jeans. When you became fashionable for the first time, even just from the waist down, you can't go back so I wore my Levi's 24/7. After about six months, bleaching jeans became fashionable and as my jeans weren't bleached, I was so last year. So late one night, when everyone else was in bed, I sneaked into the kitchen and got a bottle of Domestos and a bucket and I went out onto the veranda to bleach my jeans. The subterfuge was down to my mother telling me that I wasn't to do it because it would ruin them and money doesn't grow on trees. Technically paper is made from trees so my mother's argument was only half correct, tree wise. So there I was, furtively redesigning my jeans, when I heard hurried footsteps and saw the Orangeman running past my close with a paint-brush in his hand. It looked suspicious and it was because his pal the coach driver's car had been daubed with 1690s and FTPs.

I discovered the next day that they'd fallen out because he'd found out that the coach driver had driven Celtic supporters to a match. That's how Orange the Orangeman was. But he also wasn't the brightest lunatic bigot because he painted the bigotry on with emulsion and the coach driver managed to remove it without much difficulty. Was that the end of it? No. The following week and, bizarrely, I was out late at night on the veranda again, this time hanging my bleached jeans up in the hope of drying them overnight so I could wear them the next day to school, and this time I heard an almighty clatter and the Orangeman ran past again. This time he'd chucked an entire can of orange paint over the coach driver's car. He'd taken advice from a paint expert because he used gloss for his second attack. About a week later the Orangeman was found in his house stabbed to death. He'd been stabbed seventeen times, which even the Easterhouse police thought might actually be a murder, as opposed to the wounds being inflicted by a self-harmer. My immediate reaction was that the IRA man found him and did it but the police arrested the coach driver. After the murder and arrest both families moved away, much to the relief of everyone in the vicinity, and every time I wore my Levi's until they stopped fitting me it was a denim reminder that religion can be taken much too far.

INTO THE SEVENTIES

That spring back at school there was a serious shortage of qualified teachers and we had student teachers unleashed upon us. They'd probably hoped for a posting in Kelvinside or Newton Mearns but as their bad luck would have it they ended up in Easterhouse – the educational equivalent of cannon fodder. They just didn't have the same authority as real teachers and we knew it. The four I remember were two French students, one was Mademoiselle Menet and the other was French/Senegalese and his name was Monsieur Foch. Another was for P.E. and his name was Charles – that was his first name and he insisted we call him by it – and the fourth was a Mr Hunter who not only taught English, but also was English.

Unfortunately for Mademoiselle Menet, she had a deformed hand with very small fingers and, being completely insensitive thirteen-year-olds, we called her Fingers. Not to her face, because that would have been too completely insensitive, even for us. Monsieur Foch? Come on, what is it with the French? In primary we had Madame Anne Slack and her puppet Patapoof and now in secondary we get a teacher called Foch. It was as if they were putting obstacles in our way to stop us learning their language. Whenever a teacher was within earshot between classes in the corridor, Winker would shout Foch and when he'd been grabbed by the scruff of the neck he'd explain, 'Naw surr, I said Foch. Brown asked me what the new French student teacher's name was surr.' This was bought by every teacher except the head of French, Mr Crawford, who belted Winker for it.

Everyone from the first years up to fifth years hated getting Crawford for French because he'd give you homework, mark it out of ten, then think of a number between one and ten and everyone whose homework mark fell below the number he thought of got the belt. As for Monsieur Foch, his command of English wasn't that brilliant and Winker ended up belted again by Mr Crawford for convincing Foch that the inverted commas he'd written on the blackboard weren't called inverted commas, they were called perverted commas.

FRANKIE VAUGHAN ATE MY HAMSTER

Charles the P.E. teacher thought he was a trendy with his call-me-Charles attitude. He was also the first person I'd ever heard use terrible clichés. After one football match, when we'd been horsed by a school from Cranhill, who'd played as a team while we'd played as eleven individuals, Charles lectured us with a 'there's no I in team' speech. This was met with a direct attack on him from my teammate Wilco who said, 'No, but there's three Is in fucking idiot.' Charles also stupidly told us that he didn't believe in the belt. About a month later he did and became a major exponent of its worthiness as an aide to teaching.

Now, as shit teaching assignments go, the shittiest assignment was the organization of the end of term concert – an assignment that this particular year went to Mr Hunter. Before the break up for the summer holidays, the new intake traditionally ended the term by performing for the rest of the pupils. Hunter had to organize the first-year pupils' contribution, which meant corralling a whole first-year class, that didn't want to contribute, into some sort of passable turn. His big mistake was his misunderstanding of the relationship between Scotland and England, by which I mean that he didn't quite get the Auld Enemy thing. This led him to believe, wrongly, that we were all right behind England's bid to retain the World Cup in Mexico.

In case you'd forgotten, England won it in 1966. I thought I'd remind readers of their victory because the English may have neglected to mention it, what, since about ten minutes ago. His idea was to get the entire first year on stage to sing 'Back Home', the official England song for the 1970 World Cup, which was four years after 1966 when England won the World Cup, in England in 1966, the year England won the World Cup, in 1966.

It was a terrible idea and word got out of what the first years would be doing and the rest of the school came suitably prepared. You would have thought that other teachers would have maybe warned him of the error of his ways but they didn't, which makes me think that they were just as curious as every-one else was to find out what would happen. Come the day, the curtains went back and the entire first-year class commenced singing, 'Back home, they'll be thinking about . . .' We'd got to 'about' when the booing began and the missiles were launched. Tomatoes, clods of earth, rulers, rubbers, pencils and the likes. All during the song, which we did manage to finish, we watched teachers running up and down amongst the rows of seats, yanking out anyone who threw something. Pupils who were seen and knew they were going to get caught made sure they surrendered to a teacher who wasn't Mr McConnell. Much in the same way that the Germans in World War Two made sure they surrendered to the Allies and not to the Russians. McConnell was the last person anyone wanted the belt from. McLellan handled the largest surrender because of his ineffectual belting thanks to his arm problem. That's how my first year at secondary school ended, in a blaze of whatever the opposite of glory is.

7

FEAR AND LOATHING IN LAS PRESTWICK

The summer of 1970 was a good summer. The older generation always bang on about how it never rained and the roads were so hot they got tar stuck to their feet. Apart from the tar, that's how I remember that summer. I also remember it because it was when I bought my first single. I did have a record collection, but it was pish. It comprised of 'Two Little Boys' by Rolf Harris because my adopted Auntie Marion who lived downstairs had given me it as a present the previous Christmas and a record called 'Burning Bridges' which was the theme song from the movie *Kelly's Heroes*. My parents bought it after a visit to the flicks and I'd somehow, very much against my will, inherited it.

Buying a record was a big deal because in relative financial terms it was a big investment as we were skint. A record was 4/6d and the average pocket money was two shillings a week. So, as I say, a big investment. This meant that it took three weeks of saving to buy a record because you had to factor bus fares to and from Glasgow into the equation. I heard Dave Edmunds 'I Hear You Knocking' on the radio and I decided to buy that. Which I did, and the very next week after I bought it, it went straight to number one. I convinced myself that, as I'd bought it before it had even entered the charts, I was a 'pop picker'. Much as I loved the song, I played it so much that within three days I hated it. But that's what you did, you played it, and played it and played it, and when you got fed up with it, you turned it over to the B side and played that, and played that and played that until you got sick of that too.

FEAR AND LOATHING IN LAS PRESTWICK

That summer saw the release of Deep Purple's 'In Rock' with the cover that had the band's faces carved out à la Mount Rushmore in the States, and it is estimated, mostly by me, that Deep Purple's 'In Rock' was the LP that was carried around under the arm more than any other. People did this a) to show that they were into rock, and b) they had the Deep Purple 'In Rock' LP. This was the LP under the arm era and it seemed that everyone went round with one under their arm. I have no idea why because unless they were lugging around a Dansette and a car battery to power it, the LP couldn't be played. Perhaps it was one of those people who decided that it was indeed a ridiculous thing to do and went away and invented the iPod. Having said that, *Tomorrow's World* did indeed accurately predict that one day, music would be portable, but the future device they featured looked like a brick and probably weighed more than one. *Tomorrow's World* predicted a lot of things, of which about 1% actually panned out. The other 99% included the hover car and the jetpack we'd all be wearing to take us to work on the colony on the moon that we'd be living on.

The thing I remember most from that summer was Babs, the leader aff of the Pak, and his family moving in to the close to the left of mine, into the house vacated by the late Orangeman's family. Babs, the leader aff of a rival gang, now resided slap bang in the middle of Skinheadland. Given the way of things, this could have been considered a dangerous thing to do. But as I've previously mentioned, the Skinheads were terrified of him and I could be mistaken here, what with the mists of time, but I think they got him a house-warming present.

For some reason he asked me one day to accompany him to the bookies. Not a real bookie but a back street bookie in nearby Banton Place. You would go to the back of the close and knock on his bottom floor kitchen window, he'd open it and take the bet, all the time in shifty mode in case the police were around. The chances of the police being around were zero but he preferred to err on the side of caution. Babs won that day and decided that I was lucky, so from then on I was his mascot. For me, this meant that every time he went to the bookies I had to go with him and as long as he kept winning I'd be pretty safe. As it turned out he won all the time, although thinking back it wasn't because he was good at picking winners, it was because the bookie was too scared to tell him he wasn't winning.

Babs preferred to visit the bookies personally, but others like my Dad didn't. They laid their bets by putting a newspaper in the front window. That was the super top-secret signal recognised only by the bookies' runner who would walk about the streets looking for the signals and appear at your door to collect your line and wager.

Being under Babs's wing was like being a Made Man in the Mafia. I was untouchable and I found out how untouchable one day when we walked round a corner and encountered the Skinheads. They parted to let us through but as we walked past, one of them made a comment about my boots. My mother had bought me them and made me wear them even though they looked like the boots victims of polio had to wear because of their callipers. Babs looked straight at the one who'd made the comment and told him, 'If you've got a problem with him, you've got a problem with me.' He even made the Skinhead apologise to me. If Babs hadn't have been there, I would have had to have agreed with the Skinhead, saying, 'I know, what a wanker I am,' before limping off as though I was indeed a polio victim. The reason being, 'Yeh well, I'll bet he feels bad now, that'll teach him.'

Babs must have been about nineteen and didn't have a job. I don't suppose being the leader of a gang qualified him for much other than as leader of a gang, which is something very rarely seen in the situations vacant at the Job Centre. 'Wanted Gang Leader, must be very mental, and able to furbish references as to his mentalness.' He existed on dole money and the gang subs his gang members paid him weekly. The subs were meant to go towards paying fines but as the police never caught any of them, they therefore never ended up in court to get fined and Babs had one hell of a nest egg. Babs spent most of the summer with me and my mates sitting on the hill opposite my house. He'd regale us with stories of gang fights while chain smoking Kensitas Club and drinking El Dorado, a cheap fortified wine. Even though he was leader of a gang he never seemed to do any actual gang leading. Occasionally, a couple of the Pak would sneak into the area and he'd go off out of earshot to issue them with orders and they'd go away and he'd come back.

However, Alka, the leader aff of the Skinheads, decided that it was doing his reputation no end of harm having a rival gang's head honcho living on his turf and not having even pulled him up for it. That was the expression used; pulling someone up, that and digging someone up. One afternoon in August, Alka sent Nervo to confront Babs and tell him that Alka wanted a square go. Poor Nervo was so scared of Babs that his nervous tic was worse than it normally was and it was all he could do to stammer out the challenge. Not that it was a challenge like a gauntlet being thrown down; it was Nervo giving Babs the message, and I quote, 'Alka's gonnie rip you.' Babs looked as unbothered as I've ever seen anyone unbothered by anything and the square go was arranged for that night, the venue being the spare ground in Stepford Road adjacent to the back of the shops on Wardie Road. About half an hour later, Nervo came back to inform Babs that Alka couldn't make it that night but he re-arranged to 'rip' Babs the following week. The following week then became the following, following week and eventually never took place at all. Alka was obviously trying to call Babs bluff in the hope that he'd have declined the squarie, but he didn't and Babs reputation as a headbanger remained intact whereas Alka's reputation had gone from headbanger to total shitebag.

The only real low point of every summer was my annual family holiday. When I was thirteen my dad had got himself a car, a Morris Minor, which made everyone who got into it look a bit like Noddy. I hated the holiday fortnights away because I missed my pals, but mainly because we only ever went to a small cottage in Prestwick or to a caravan at Maidens. Even before the new M77 was built, Prestwick was still only about forty minutes away, so as a holiday it was hardly a far-flung destination, it was just down the road a bit. Maidens was slightly further away with another nine minutes on from Prestwick to reach Maybole and a further three minutes via Maybole into Maidens. Even on daytrips to either destination it's hard to find something to do to fill an afternoon but fourteen afternoons, fourteen mornings and fourteen nights? Forget it.

The most exciting thing that ever happened to me at Prestwick was finding a dead seal washed up on the beach, and the hours of fun I had poking it with a stick. That aside, Prestwick was an evil place because it had an outdoor swimming pool and it was the reason why Prestwick's population has never increased. Any man who swam in the freezing water lost the use of his testicles for the rest of the year. It was also used by scientists carrying out experiments in cryogenics. Ten seconds in the pool was enough to completely freeze a human body. This leads me to believe that Walt Disney must have been cryogenically frozen using Prestwick's open-air pool. I did learn to swim in that pool but only because my dad plonked me in the shallow end and told me if I could make it to the other end I could get out. I was like Rebecca Adlington, only faster. In fact I was like a torpedo, a torpedo with hypothermia.

Admittedly, Prestwick also had a boating pond, and that's fine if you owned a toy boat. I didn't. It also had a putting green, a penny arcade and go-karts. Putting is boring, you ran out of pennies in about four minutes which dropped to two minutes if you played the Penny Fountain, and the go-karts were out of my price range. So, wandering about aimlessly was about it for Prestwick with the occasional High Tea to look forward to. Fish and chips, with peas, a cup of tea and two slices of bread.

That was considered a really special treat. Who would think that a special treat, Bobby Sands?

Maidens was a whole different ball game. These holidays usually comprised of sitting in a caravan taking a coma while the rain battered off the roof. Maidens had no facilities at all so there was even less than nothing to do – nothing apart from sitting on the harbour with a small wooden fishing frame with orange nylon fishing rope. The whole harbour was dotted with bored Glaswegian kids sitting, not catching anything with the fishing frame because no one had ever caught anything using them. I'm sure the people in the shop facing the harbour used to piss themselves laughing while watching us all. More than likely they had great time saying, 'Look at those Glaswegians trying to catch fish, fucking idiots.'

The day we arrived on any holiday I counted down the days until it was over. I stopped short from marking the wall on the caravan with a nail like convicts count down the years in prison, but only because we would have had to pay for the damage. Once it was over, my Dad would pack the unused deck chairs and the case into the car and we'd head back to Easterhouse and I was never as glad to see anywhere as I was then. We returned with stalks of rock with the names Prestwick or Maidens running through them and would hand them out with a card with the name of a good dentist on it.

8

HUSH HUSH

Back at school, it was time to start second year. Not straight into school I hasten to add. All the ex-first years, who were now second years, hung around the gate to watch what – if anything – would be inflicted on the new intake. This year the headmaster had got it right and the area was patrolled by teachers and jannies so no one suffered anything, which was nice for them, albeit hugely disappointing for us. We were also there to check out the female intake for talent. It was common knowledge that girls only fancied pupils of the year above, as dating someone in your own year was considered uncool. As we were now second years, we assumed every first-year female would fancy us.

Puberty was kicking in and with it came an interest in the opposite sex but in the age of innocence we had all our facts totally wrong. Sex education was a thing of the future and in those days we had to discover things for ourselves. For instance, we thought a poof was a cow's joabie, because . . . when a cow did its business the result was something resembling a pouffe chair. Made perfect sense to us! It was only when Winker wrote 'Franny McCafferty is a Poof' in the mud during a football match and Franny's big brother gave him a kicking for it whilst explaining to him what a poof was did we find out what it actually meant.

We had this mate Billy Tonagh who was a couple of years older than us and he told us his brother had done 'it' with a girl. His brother had explained to him the process and now he was relaying it to us second hand. He told us that a man puts his thing next to a woman's thing and they got this wee electric shock and that was it, dead simple.

One of the assembled listeners took the whole thing quite literally and thought all that he was missing was the electricity. So he got his father's old car battery out of a cupboard and jump-started himself with a set of jump leads. He ended up in hospital but his name said it all – Willie Burns. We were so naive that we didn't even know what the derogatory term 'wanker' that we applied to everyone actually meant. All we knew was that every time we used it in the classroom we were given the belt.

The sex discussion continued and we all jumped in with snippets of knowledge. Eddie had been leafing through his mother's catalogue, the bra section to be exact, and discovered what breasts were for thanks to a picture featuring a front opening bra for breast-feeding. That's not how he put it though. He told us that a woman's diddies served the same function as a cow's bagpipes.

In 1971, I saw my first unfettered boobs. Okay, they were on a cinema screen and the owner of them was dead and was being fished out of a swimming pool, but I'm sure it still counts. Four of us decided that we'd try and get in to see *Dirty Harry* at the ABC cinema in Shettleston. We were fourteen and *Dirty Harry* was an X-rated movie, but Barry Norman said it was brilliant on Film '71 and we thought it was worth a shot. We dressed as adult as we could and got the bus into Shettleston early on Saturday night. There was me, Eddie, Wilco and a guy called Bobby Thomlinson who we never went around with much because he wore a lot of crushed velvet and had bumfluff. Our thinking was he could get the tickets because, thanks to the bumfluff on his face, he looked much, much older than the fourteen-years-old that he was. He looked maybe fifteen, almost fifteen and a half. We arrived and we hung back while he approached the ticket booth because we hoped we'd look older from further away. We needn't have bothered because the worker manning the booth couldn't give a toss and Bobby bought the tickets without even a cursory 'what age are you lot' to at least look as though he was trying a wee bit to adhere to the British Film Board censorship ratings. We went upstairs and sat down and the first scene was the dead boobs scene and we thought, 'Wow, so that's what they look like.' The movie did later on show another pair of boobs but they belonged to a fat ugly woman and they definitely didn't count. I'm just wondering how many people can say that they saw their first ever boobs in Shettleston. Actually, it's probably a lot more people than you'd think.

After the second year 'hello again' assembly, we were given our timetables and a double period of algebra was my welcome back to Westwood. I hated algebra because I just could not understand it and neither, despite his enormous intellect, could Winker. The teacher, Mr Russell, explained to us as best he could the workings of the subject. We just stared at him because it all sounded like gibberish.

Once, after banging on for about ten minutes on the principles, Winker put his hand up and said, 'So fuck.'

Russell looked at him and decided that any reaction was better than no reaction at all and added that we could apply algebra in later life when we had secured gainful employment. Winker's hand went up again.

'What as, sir, fucking astronauts?'

Russell gave him the belt. Too much reaction.

The Maths teacher's nickname was Tranny because he was hard of hearing and wore one of the giant pre-digital hearing aids, which made it look like he'd a transistor radio stuck to his head. Some pupils, not me, used to silently mouth answers to questions he'd asked them and because he could see their lips moving but couldn't hear anything he would fiddle with his hearing aid because he thought it wasn't working. It was just as well he couldn't lip read because the answers they were giving him were wrong anyway.

Other subjects, too, seemed totally pointless, like Physics for instance. What was the reasoning of time in motion, a small-wheeled object running down a slope, attached to tick-ertape, to tell us its speed in comparison to its mass weight? Another 'what as, sir, fucking astronauts' moment.

To this day I have no concept of algebra. X plus Y equals Z, whatever Z is, and I have never used algebra or physics for anything ever. Not even once.

In September, we were offered the chance to go away for a week to the school's camp in Millport. All we had to do to qualify was to get our parents to sign a form saying that, in the event of us not returning in one piece, the school couldn't be held responsible. My parents signed the form with undue haste.

Millport was over the sea, well a wee bit anyway, and we were all really excited. Twenty-four of us were to go, plus Mr Menzies and a Miss Campbell. Roy Jones, the language lab technician, was going too. It was thought that the headmaster had sent him along to keep an eye on Menzies and Campbell because he suspected they were having an inter-staff relation-ship, which he frowned upon.

We set off in the school minibus bright and early one Monday morning. Roy was driving and us bad boys were sitting at the back as far away as possible from the alleged lovebirds who were occupying the front seats. The girls occupied the rest of the front half of the bus.

We spent the first half of the journey giving two fingers to any motorist who was unfortunate enough to be travelling behind us. We just did the two-fingered thing because the middle finger thing hadn't reached the UK from America. But there are only so many times you can flick the Vs before it gets boring and after fifteen minutes it did. Everyone was in high spirits and inevitably the singing started. We, being the 'lads', refused to join in so the girls started singing.

'The back of the bus they cannae sing, they cannae sing, they cannae . . .'

They were interrupted by Eddie who stood up mid-chorus and shouted over their dulcet tones, 'Naw but we can fight like fuck.'

Menzies was not a pleased man as he had hoped for a week of peace and quiet to continue with his wooing of Miss Campbell. He reckoned the outburst was a portent of things to come and realised he had gone away with the children of the damned. He decided to try a new approach with us, as he knew that threats and violence would not work, so he gave us his 'little adults' speech.

'Right, that's enough, we are all grown up here and it's about time we acted like it. We have left the confines and the constraints of the school and we are going to have a pleasant week. We are going as friends, not as teachers and pupils, now you can call me Colin this week, Miss Campbell's name is Linda and you all know Roy, so let's be little adults.'

Winker thought the prospect over for a minute or two.

'Colin.'

'Yes Winker.'

'Are you gonnie be spending the week trying to slip Linda the mitt?'

We arrived at the place the school called Hush Hush. It had been a secret naval base during the war and the name had stuck.

As soon as the minibus had stopped we went off to explore but that took us just about ten minutes, as Millport, apart from being a lovely wee scenic place, really has nothing else but a bit of scenery.

The whole place seemed to be full of rabbits running around banging into things. We returned to base and asked Roy the question, 'Hey, how come all the rabbits here are pure pished?'

Roy told us that they weren't pished, they were suffering from myxomatosis, a disease given to them by man to stop them breeding and overrunning the island. Winker suggested that maybe Colin should be given a dose of it to control his plan to breed with Linda. Roy laughed, he had a sense of humour. He was about twenty and as he had just qualified, he hadn't yet achieved the distance of the pupil and employee of the education department relationship.

HUSH HUSH

Our first night in Hush Hush was spent in the sleepless pursuit of trying to get into the girls' dorm. What we would have done once we'd managed to sneak in was a mystery but we felt we'd be letting ourselves down if we didn't at least try.

At breakfast the next day Colin gave us the entertainment schedule. Day one we were to go into the town and hire bicycles, which we would then use to ride round the island, wooo – such excitement. I asked him why we just couldn't go round the island in the minibus, which prompted a dirty look and a lecture about fresh air in the lungs. Roy was given the task of driving us into town as Colin and Linda were staying behind to prepare the evening meal.

Roy dropped us off and disappeared into the pub. He gave us two hours to do the circumnavigation of the island tour and said he would then meet us back at the hire shop. We got on our bikes and headed back in the direction we had just come. It was about five miles back to Hush Hush and we called the rally the 'let's catch them with their knickers round their ankles' cycle race.

We cycled back like demons, cackling like maniacs as we went. We got back and they were indeed preparing the evening meal. Colin was sitting outside peeling potatoes. He did how-ever have a glow of smug satisfaction about him so we did wonder.

We goaded Colin the best way we could for the first couple of days and he took it in surprisingly good humour. It was only later we found out that he was just biding his time. Like a Martian in H. G. Wells's *War of the Worlds* – slowly and surely he laid his plans against us.

On the third night he appeared at the hut door carrying a fishing net and a torch. He then made a great play of acting casually. We feigned disinterest until he selected a log and began to bang it off the floor. Satisfied with his choice, he went outside and we followed him out as curiosity had now got the better of us.

'Colin, what's the gear for?'

He told us that he was going to hunt Bull Rabbits for the next day's dinner. Hunting, now this was more like it. But what was a Bull Rabbit and how are they caught? Colin explained.

'They are male rabbits about twice the size as normal, they are nocturnal, and they can easily be identified by their large antlers.

'The way to catch them is to run along the road stretching the net across it. The Bull Rabbits will be stunned by the torchlight, and stand so still that it's incredibly easy to crack them over the skull with the log.'

Being from the city, and not too well versed in the flora and fauna of our native country, we believed him and the prospect of satisfying our schoolboy bloodlust was far too much for us. We asked if we could have a go. He handed us the equipment and sat on the entrance gate and watched us charge off down the road.

There were about ten of us running along the dark roads and screaming our heads off. Winker was following with the torch and Eddie was behind him with the log. Every so often a car would come along driven by a local. They'd slow down to look at the bizarre scene of ten smiling loonies armed with a net, a torch and a log. Once they had decided that we must be mad they would speed off, leaving skid marks and the smell of burning rubber.

We must have run for a couple of miles before we decided that the Bull Rabbits were in bed and dejectedly we made our way back to Hush Hush. On the way back, the torch batteries ran out and every so often one of us would yell out expletives as we fell into a ditch. We reached Hush Hush to find the place strangely silent and in total darkness. We approached cautiously and edged our way through the door.

All the lights went on and Colin was standing with all the females who were screaming and laughing. We'd been had. Well and truly had.

Colin was beyond smug as he had made us look like total

idiots in the eyes of the girls, not only that but he'd probably raised his self-esteem with his 'burd'.

Waking early the next morning, we convened a war cabinet behind the main hut and decided we'd have to be come up with something clever to pay him back for making us look like tubes.

Winker came up with a plan.

We made a dummy out of clothes and stuffed it with grass and straw, for an added touched of reality we used a turnip for its head with Winker's Rangers tammy on it as the final touch. We did debate whether or not the Rangers tammy was a good idea because Menzies might be a Celtic fan and wouldn't lift a finger to save a Rangers fan from drowning. We decided he wasn't a Celtic fan, for no other reason than we were pretty sure Menzies wasn't a Catholic sounding name. Eddie said he was convinced he wasn't a Catholic because 'he doesnae look like one'. Since we didn't exactly know what that meant we took Eddie at his word. I mean it's not as if he went about dressed like the Pope.

From a distance the dummy looked quite lifelike. We took it out to the shoreline amongst the rocks and put it in the water. After letting it drift out about twenty yards, Eddie ran into the hut screaming that Winker had fallen in, banged his head and was now in the advanced stages of drowning.

Colin came running out, quickly surveyed the situation and waded in to rescue the dummy. He actually looked quite heroic. It would have been more heroic if he'd dived in, but I suppose wading in was still sort of heroic-ish.

It was only on reaching the dummy he realised he'd been duped and we all started cheering. He waded back, got out, dripped his way past us and back off into the hut to dry off. We'd had our revenge and decided to call it quits.

On our last night anyone who wanted was allowed to go into the town unaccompanied. Only four of us took up the offer, the rest wanted to stay and sing songs round the campfire that Colin was building.

Roy drove us in and disappeared off into the pub.

Eddie, Winker, Wilco and myself found this cafe and went in for some soft drinks. A few of the local kids sat about and every so often one of them threw us a dirty look. Not that this bothered us at first, as we were from Easterhouse and thought we were dead tough, but eventually it became annoying and Eddie asked them, 'What do you think you are looking at ya pricks?'

He elongated the word pricks, so it sounded more like pricksaaaaaaaaaa. He thought the extra long 'a' sounded scarier.

One of the locals said, 'Nothing,' and Eddie said, 'Aye, ye'd fucking better not be.'

There were only three of them and we were four, not bad odds in the event of things turning nasty. We soon got bored with the cafe and walked outside and up towards the pier. The locals came out and followed us. Winker looked back and said, 'What's their problem?'

It wasn't their problem, it was ours. All along the walk they were joined by more locals coming out of houses, which was impressive because it was long before the age of mass communication and it's not as if they texted or tweeted each other. I can only figure that they were all telepathic and that's how the message that strangers were in town was passed around. By the time we got to the pier, there were about twenty of them ranging from about four-years-old to about sixteen-years-old. One of them only had one leg and was using crutches.

Once on the pier we were trapped, there was only one way out and that was to jump off the pier and swim to Largs or go through them.

'What now?' asked Winker.

Eddie was in no mood to back down and he took a step towards them, threatening, 'What are youse looking at?' He had his hand in his jacket as though he was concealing a weapon. His hope was that this looked threatening. They didn't answer him. They just stood there staring at us and their silence was a bit freaky. Winker took a couple of steps towards them and they stepped back. 'They're fucking shitebags, mon then, come intae us.' He held up both hands and was beckoning them with his fingertips to come forward. The biggest one spoke: 'We're the Millport Young Team.'

'Wooooooo,' said Eddie, 'the Millport Young Team. Well yeez urnae going to live long enough to be the Millport Old Team, so come on, are we going right ahead or whit.'

Eddie whispered to us, 'Act mental and they'll shit themselves.'

We started shouting names at them and generally looking as though we weren't right in the heads. I am ashamed to say it felt good. Four against twenty and they were looking very apprehensive and stood there not knowing what to do.

Obviously they couldn't back down and by this stage, neither could we.

The deadlock was broken when the only cop on the island turned up in his Panda car and they scattered.

We stood our ground.

'Right, what's going on here?'

'It was them, they followed us.'

'I assume you lot are from Hush Hush?'

'Aye.'

'Is there anyone with you?'

'The language lab guy, he's in the pub.'

'Wait here and I'll go and get him.'

Roy was pissed off at being dragged out of the pub and drove us back in silence. We told him it wasn't our fault but he just ignored us after saying, 'Yeh right.'

We got back to Hush Hush and found everyone sitting round a huge bonfire singing campfire type songs. Boring!!!!! Especially after our night out.

The next morning we piled into the minibus and headed homeward.

When Roy started up the engine there was a cheer – only Colin and Linda looked unhappy at the prospect of returning to the headmaster's moral regime.

9

ASPIRIN AND COKE

Apart from the trip to Hush Hush, nothing of any note happened in 1970 or 1971, but when 1972 kicked in, things were in a transformation. Fashion became ridiculous. We already had flares but only hippies and pop stars wore them. Now we had something much, much worse – baggie trousers. They were thirty inches wide at the thigh and thirty inches wide at the bottom. The comic look was worsened by a nine-inch waistband. The really fashion conscious glitterati had theirs made to measure by a tailor in Glasgow city centre called Arthur Black. Anyone with enough cash could be made into a clown.

Our school uniform had changed from Gloverall Dufflecoats and a pair of Levi's to Gloverall Dufflecoats and thirty-inch bags, and the Headmaster put his foot down. He gathered us all together in the hall and lectured us on the etiquette of the school uniform. Up until this point he had been quite liberal but now he had decided enough was enough. Anyone appearing in the school in 'Oxford Bags' would be sent home.

The next day there were a lot of clowns wandering the streets very aimlessly.

The way we dressed was also influenced by music. Slade fans, for instance, wore Doc Martens, denim jackets and sported skinhead haircuts, while Heavy Rock fans wore Doc Martens, denim jackets and sported long hair. Note once again the subtle difference. The other footwear available were Monkey Boots and Sacha platforms, the latter of which were girls' shoes but because they were only £13.99, as opposed to the £90 custom-made platforms you could order at Slack Shack in Argyle Street, they were worn by both sexes. I was chased one night by the West Rebels when I was wearing my Sachas and obviously I couldn't really run, luckily for me they were wearing their Sachas too. The scene must have looked ridiculous with me taking tiny wee steps like a Geisha girl and them taking tiny wee steps like a gang of Geisha girls. I managed to escape because it suddenly dawned on me that I could take them off and run in my bare feet.

For my birthday that year I was given money. New fancy decimal money, and with my new fancy decimal money I decided I wanted a customised jersey from Argyle House, a shop at the top of Buchanan Street, which for decimal money, or any money at all, would give you any design you wanted. I wanted a jersey zipper with tartan patches and my name on it, which by that time I had changed from Richie to Rikki. So I collected my birthday money and got the bus into the Buchanan Street bus station. I went into the shop and explained to the woman behind the desk what I wanted. She noted all this down and I told her that as a finishing touch I wanted Rikki knitted into the panel of the left breast. She told me that this would be £1 extra as it was twenty new pennies per letter. The problem was that I only had 80p left so I had to drop one of the Ks. A fortnight later I collected it and was chuffed to bits because I thought it looked really cool. But the first time I wore it Eddie looked at the jersey and said, 'You're a prick, you cannae even spell your own fucking name.' Needless to say I never wore it ever again.

Music was becoming an important part of our lives but our tastes were divided. Some of us liked one thing, others something else. I recall one night going up to this guy Shuggie MacMillan's house because he said he'd the best record ever recorded. And that turned out to be, in his opinion, Jimi Hendrix's 'Voodoo Chile'. Admittedly it is a classic, but he ruined it by every ten seconds excitedly pointing out an on-coming guitar solo and trying to play along with it on a poxy Spanish guitar with nylon strings that his mother had got him for his Christmas.

Hendrix fans were a breed apart from the rest of us. They were the people who would scrape off the insides of the banana peel and smoke it saying, '*What a high man.*' I did try it but it never worked for me. I was told I didn't have the right vibes for a hit. They also put Aspirin into Coke because they said this gave them a high. It more than likely didn't and just gave them an Aspirin and Coke. Drugs didn't really exist, at least that's how I remember it, unless I was on drugs at the time and that's why I can't remember drugs existing. No, they didn't, that was a problem that was far off.

New words started appearing in our language, words such as 'far out', a derivative of 'far off'. There was also 'heavieee', and 'stoned'. In Easterhouse it caused a lot of confusion, if one were to say, 'I'm gonnie get stoned the night,' it either meant that one would be partaking of a banana roll up or had the intention of walking down the wrong street and criticising the local gang leader.

Being in a group became the cool thing to do. All the girls were into pop stars and 99% of them had 'I Love Marc Bolan' written on their schoolbooks and schoolbags. With that in mind we decided to start a band with the idea of seeing our names on their schoolbags.

We had our first meeting in a guy called Kenny's house. Kenny was a year younger than us but he had a big brother in a band and the equipment was stashed in his house. We knew this, befriended him and asked him to join us.

At our first meeting we discussed the stuff we would play and who would play what. Kenny said he would be the lead guitarist, Eddie on drums, Wilco on rhythm, Winker on vocals and me on bass. We visited the Congregational Church fifty yards along the road from Kenny's house and asked the minister if we could rehearse in the hall. Being a kindly soul he agreed as long we didn't break or steal anything.

We approached this particular church because it was the church my mother went to and as the minister knew our family, he unfortunately agreed by using the shortened version of my Sunday name of Richard, which I was only ever called by my Dad. 'Of course you can Dick.' Wilco said he wasn't really surprised because he always thought I was a dick. It took me years to live that down. Why are so many names words for sexual organs? There's Dick, Willie, Boaby and Nobby, and not wanting to appear sexist, there's Fanny and Nan too. It just isn't right. Parents should really think about what they call their kid, they should check it can't be shortened or messed about with to something that can leave a permanent scar. Then again every Dick, Willie and Boaby have got off lightly compared with the couple from Possil who christened their poor kid Pocahontas.

We carted all the stuff along from Kenny's house and set it up.

'Right,' said Kenny, 'we'll start with Free's "All Right Now".'

Kenny hit the first few chords while the rest of just looked at each other. Kenny stopped playing, 'What? Do you not know it then?

'Aye, we know it but we don't fucking know how to play it.'

Kenny looked at us.

Winker piped up, 'I know the words.'

Eddie added, 'So what, we all know the words.'

Kenny said, 'Okay it's basically just the chords C, G and F, then the rest is simple.'

Wilco asked him, 'So what's a chord then?'

Kenny put his Fender Stratocaster down. 'Can any of you lot actually play anything?' He directed the question to Wilco and myself.

'Well naw, no really.'

Kenny had a look of puzzlement on his face. 'Well how the fuck can we start a band then?'

Eddie hit a drum a few times. 'Well this bit's a fucking dawdle.'

Winker said, 'Knowing the words must be a start as well.'

Kenny went on to explain the principles of being in a group and that being able to play something was pretty high up on the list. He added that he had been playing the guitar for three years and it was not an easy thing to play well.

After a lot of cajoling he agreed to teach us and within three weeks we had just about learned to play one number badly. Fame was just around the corner. We were just in the process of learning our second number when Kenny's big brother's band went on tour and took their equipment with them. That was the end of our musical aspirations, albeit temporarily. But it was just as well, as most rehearsal nights we were joined by Kenny's pal Scraggs and his girlfriend, and if Scraggs wasn't stealing chocolate bars belonging to the Church's playgroup, which were stored in the kitchen, he was up in the pulpit with his girlfriend winching the face off her. Now I'm not really all that religious but somehow I just felt that using the pulpit for winching was something that the Good Lord himself might just frown upon. And God knew exactly what was going on because God is omnipresent. Seemingly he's like Santa in that respect.

Despite our attempts to create our own amusement, there was not much for entertainment around Easterhouse, for, aside from all the social ills, the biggest problem Easterhouse had was a lack of facilities. It was fine if you wanted a newspaper, which you could get from Pat O'Neil's, one of four shops on Wardie Road. It was also fine if you wanted milk because then you were spoilt for choice between Templeton's and the Co-op, and if you fancied a chop for your tea, the fourth shop was the butcher's. Other than that, anything else meant a bus ride into Glasgow. But now, in 1972, the Shopping Centre opened.

It was supposed to have been built many years earlier but there were said to be mine workings under the whole of Easterhouse and no one would take the responsibility for the centre ending up disappearing down a mineshaft. Eventually someone in authority decided, 'Aw for god's sake stop fannying about and build the thing,' and it was built.

When it was finished it really wasn't the shopping metropolis everyone had been hoping for. In fact, it seemed to only cater to an older generation because it had a Galls Wool Shop that sold wool, knitting needles and patterns. Also, when Fine Fayre got around to opening their supermarket within the mall, they got Moira Anderson to cut the ribbon. For younger readers, Moira Anderson was the Cheryl Cole of her day. But only if Cheryl Cole was a big posh wumman who sung traditional Scottish songs. No offence to Moira Anderson, who I know to be a lovely woman because I met her years later when I was the writer on a comedy quiz show which celebrated BBC Scotland's 75th anniversary, but come on, Moira Anderson? My theory was that someone wanted to find out how many pensioners lived in Easterhouse and the best way to get them all together in one place at the same time to count them was to announce that Moira Anderson will be at the Fine Fayre at 3pm on Friday. I think the posters read 'Meet Moira, Buy Some Wool', and if they didn't, they should have.

All the OAP's crowded in and for health and safety reasons all the doors had to be left open to help ventilate the place because of the overwhelming stench of perm lotion. Having said that, it was the first fully enclosed, air-conditioned shopping mall in Scotland. The ideal place to shop when the temperature outside reaches a phew, pure boiling sixty-two degrees. It was also the proud owner of a terrazzo floor. And everyone thought, 'That's brilliant, a terrazzo floor . . . by the way, what's a terrazzo floor?'

Easterhouse today has a new giant shopping centre called the Easterhouse Fort. If they are trying to regenerate the place with a new message of hope for the future, isn't calling the centre after a building where people would gather together for safety just taking the piss?

The original mall was built amongst a group of other new

buildings collectively known as the Township Centre, the foundation stone of which was laid by the Right Honourable Dr J. Dickson Mabon, Member of Parliament and Minister of State. He laid the stone in 1969 and by the time they'd announced his full name and titles it was 1972 and the project was finished. The Township Centre included swimming baths, a Labour Exchange and a very busy Social Work Department. The Township Centre boasted spaces for over 200 cars – 100 burnt out and 100 on bricks with the wheels missing.

A year later in 1973, the police station opened and this allowed the police to respond to call outs a lot quicker than they had in the past. It was estimated that, being within the close vicinity, the cops could now knock a whole five minutes off their usual three-hour response time.

There was also now a library that contained books. In 1972 in Easterhouse, the reaction to that was: 'Books? . . . naw you've lost me.' The library only existed because local women had lobbied the council. Basically local activist women, the ones who always start a public statement by saying, 'Well, speaking as a wumman putting on a voice . . .' The statement usually made for a library was, 'Aye, ma wean has got tae go all the way tae Shettleston tae knock books, and that's just no good enough ne'er it is, is that no right Betty hen.' The reason Betty is mentioned is because they all had a pal called Betty who they took with them to back them up.

I'm joking about the not knowing what books were thing because everyone could read, at least everyone I knew could. They had to able to read to fill in buroo claim forms. And my friends and I spent many a happy hour reading the Glasgow Parks Department rules sign at the entrance to Blairtummock Park. The rule we read most while sniggering like schoolboys, which we were, was the one that said, 'No prostitution.' Not that the Parks Department thought that hookers would ever ply their trade in Blairtummock Park but they were just covering every eventuality. The only way they could have plied their trade in Easterhouse would have been if they accepted Provi cheques. Then again, if hookers ever did fancy a change from Blythswood Square, they could solicit with impunity because another rule was no drinking in the park and that was really all the park was mostly ever used for.

To further enhance community spirit, some residents' committee or other started an Easterhouse festival complete with a girl who'd been crowned the Easterhouse Queen. They didn't want to call her Miss Easterhouse because that might have sounded more like an instruction to taxi drivers. On the opening day of the week-long Gala, the Easterhouse Queen was driven round the scheme on the back of a coal lorry that had been cleaned up for the day. She'd be driven about waving at poor people. Who did she think she was, the Pope?

During the festival many free events were held and the events must have been pretty bad because I cannot remember a single one. I have my suspicions, though, that there were a lot of cookery demonstrations, exhibitions of knitting and church socials with tea and biscuits. The local MP Hugh Brown did turn up during the festival and shook a few hands, but only after insisting they were scrubbed with Dettol first.

Easterhouse was staunchly a Labour area. Always has been, always will be, but surely if people want things done in Scotland they should vote Tory? Of course, the Tories do nothing for Scotland, why should they? No one votes for them, so Scotland doesn't count. I firmly believe that we should vote Conservative even if we don't really mean it because if we did, they'd be a lot less apt to ignore our problems if we actually meant the difference between winning and losing an election.

What did change Easterhouse for the better wasn't shopping, or political will, or new swimming baths, a library, an Easterhouse Queen or a social works department megastore. It was the new M8 motorway that changed the landscape forever.

The Monklands canal, known locally as the Nolly, was filled in and the M8 followed its path. This cut Easterhouse in half and made it harder for the gangs to move so freely about because it wasn't easy charging across a motorway to fight their rivals. Not with cars belting along it at 70mph and them trying to avoid getting run over like the frog crossing the road video game. Beforehand, two-lane road bridges spanned the Nolly and they allowed easy access but after the motorway was finished, only narrow foot bridges spanned the M8. Bridges so narrow that one gang member armed with an empty Irn Bru bottle could have held it for weeks. Any gang trying to take the bridge from him would have taken hundreds of casualties before realising that it was a bridge too far.

During the building of the motorway the engineers would periodically use dynamite and its use was preceded by a warning siren. This didn't really have the desired effect of clearing the area but led to people rushing to a distance they deemed reasonably safe to watch the explosions. A pensioner three closes down from ours reacted differently to the siren. She'd lived through the war and whenever she heard it she'd hide under her living room table crying and shouting, 'Bert . . . Bert, the bloody Germans . . . Bert.' Thinking back, it really wasn't safe because rubble would fly for hundreds of yards always just narrowly missing terrified cows in the fields adjacent to the M8's route, so maybe the OAP was right, perhaps the contractors were bloody Germans. I must ask Bert, if I ever find out who Bert is.

10

SINGLE AND A MATCH

Being a fast runner in a Glasgow scheme meant one of two things. Either you'd trained as an athlete, or you'd trained as a shitebag. The former, if you were fast enough, helped win you medals and the latter, if you were fast enough, helped you outrun whichever gang happened to be chasing you. Running was never really seen as a sport because the general attitude was a sarcastic 'wow, you can put one foot in front of the other and propel yourself forward a wee bit faster than other people can, you're brilliant, I wish I was you'.

Not that my school had that many 'athletes'. When I say not many I mean we had one. His name was John Tucker, but he only became a runner and a pretty good runner too because he was absolutely crap at football. Every time the ball went anywhere near him he let out an involuntary squeal, panicked, swung at it and completely missed. But during the sports days held on the last day before the summer break he won every event. He never lost, because it would have been hard to lose to the fellow competitors in the 800 metres who'd run the first 200 metres, given up and walked the remaining 600 metres smoking fags.

The sports day was always an afterthought and only ever mentioned the day before at assembly when the headmaster would dismiss us after the Lord's Prayer and then say, 'Oh hold on, I almost forgot, tomorrow is our annual sports day.' The preparations consisted of the janitor tying the only twenty feet of bunting the school possessed to the mesh fence next to the track. The small Union Jacks were so old and faded that I don't even think they were left over from V.E. Day. My guess would be that they were left over from a street party to celebrate the lifting of the Siege of Mafeking.

Equal lack of preparation went into deciding who would run and the competitors would be picked, not on the basis of athletic ability, but on the basis of who was standing closest to the teacher when he was deciding who would do what. During my first two years at secondary my mates and I buggered off as soon as the events started but in third year the girls in my class had started to develop breasts so we hung around to see what they looked like when they were running, and we weren't disappointed. When you're fifteen, 32As are an incredibly big deal.

The annual Sports Day aside, sport at my school was always a double period of football, usually unsupervised because the P.E. teachers would divide you into two teams, hand you bibs and a ball and tell you to beat it. Of course no one wanted to go in goals but that was settled democratically by a vote in which the only candidate for that position was the fat kid who always won by a landslide, which he'd probably caused anyway by falling over his fat feet. Fat kids got stuck in goals because that was the natural order of things. If a fat kid refused to go in goals we threatened that we'd treat him like Piggy and get all *Lord of the Flies* on him. The *Lord of the Flies* threat was actually very good news for the education system because it meant we'd read a book.

Without the existence of fat kids, each class as I recall had two, every match would have been played without a goalie. I'm pretty sure this had been taken into consideration when pupils were being allocated classes on arrival at secondary school because the fat kids would be separated, weighed and counted to ensure that each class contained the required tonnage in goalkeeping quota. In those less enlightened times every fat kid's Christian name was replaced with Fatso and they'd go through their entire secondary education with that moniker. That's just how it was. If you had buckteeth you were called Bugsy, acne sufferers got called Spotty and if you were a wanker you got called Wanker. It wasn't meant to be nasty, it was meant to be descriptive.

The sad thing with the fat kids is that they probably were overweight through no fault of their own and did indeed suffer from a glandular problem. Fast food didn't exist in Easterhouse and the closest chippie was a bus ride away in Shettleston and by the time you'd walked to the bus stop to get the bus there and from the bus stop when you got back you'd have burnt up the fish supper calories anyway. The health Nazis didn't exist in the seventies either as it was only a mere decade after doctors were still insisting that smoking was good for you. I have a football programme from 1972 which features full page adverts for both Rothmans and Regal King size, and a double page spread devoted to the entire Tennent's range of products including Charger Lager, Hemelling, Tennent's Extra and Super, Lamot Pilsner, Breaker Malt and their alcohol-free lager Barbican.

Barbican didn't sell very well because not only was it alcohol free, it was also alcohol free. Just two of the reasons no one bought it. If someone had the audacity to criticise your diet, your drinking or especially your smoking with the 'you are taking years off your life' speech, their lives would have ended prematurely too – seconds after they'd finished their health Nazi lecture. We are talking about a time when the ice cream van not only sold ice cream but for 3d they'd sell you a single and a match. That is a single cigarette and a match to light it with. We are also talking a time when no one bought a kettle, a chip pan or an ironing board with money. Everyone acquired such items by smoking Kensitas Club to collect the coupons, which then would be exchanged for household goods and little luxuries in the Kensitas Club shop located above the Grand Fare in Cambridge Street. For 500 coupons you could get a kettle, 700 a chip pan, 800 an ironing board and for 20,000 a brand new pair of lungs.

Life expectancy still isn't that great in the East End of Glasgow and according to the United Nation's Health Committee, the average person in the East End can expect to live slightly longer than a gangster rapper, but slightly less than an IRA informer.

Each football team consisted of the fat kid in goals and ten centre forwards, which basically meant two packs of ten running after the ball in an assortment of ill-suited footwear. If you were very lucky you had football boots, but most people played in sandshoes that had all the support of ladies pop socks, or in school shoes or Doc Martens. We never had strips, except on school team match days when we were handed a stinking top each that hadn't seen the inside of a washing machine in months. In most cases it was only the crap on them that held them together. The smell was indescribable – actually it isn't. Think of the disgusting public toilet stench of fusty urine and mix that with the disgusting stench of urinal cake. Double that by a million, and that's about half as bad as the stink was. Flies would fly close and then buzz off quickly saying, 'Jeez oh, that's even too much for me, I'm off to soak up the aroma of a much more fragrant dog shite.'

Football back then was a brutal contact sport and the only way you could get yourself sent off was if you'd concealed a claw hammer about your person and felled an opponent with the business end of it. If you weren't the victim of a random act of violence, or a fair tackle as it was called, then the playing surface would get you.

Playing on grass was almost unheard of as most school pitches were red ash, a surface on which a sliding tackle left you requiring a skin graft. Sometimes the wound was so bad that you had to visit the hospital where the doctor would take one look at it and phone the police to report they are dealing with a patient who'd been tied to a car bumper and dragged along the road for miles. Red ash though was a luxurious velvet cushion compared to a black ash pitch, which was made of crushed volcanic matter. I say crushed but it was never crushed as much as it should have been. This meant it started the season as 50% ash and 50% sharp chards but ended the season as 40% ash, 40% sharp chards and 20% bone, muscle and skin tissue.

We did have grass in Easterhouse, but you weren't allowed to play football on it. The council had erected signs on every patch of grass that read 'No Ball Games'. I think they didn't want their grass hurt. Dogs could crap on it, you could smash glass on it, you could even stab someone on it, but if you went anywhere near it with a ball, the police would come and arrest you. This happened to my brother and his pals when they were caught by two undercover cops. That it wasn't deemed a waste of police resources to have two undercover cops staking out a small patch of grass shows the mentality of most of the police in Easterhouse at the time.

'But officers, there's a man getting stabbed over there.'

'Stabbings are ten a penny son, what you lot are doing is far more serious, it's heinous.'

They were lifted and taken to the police station by the undercover cops who'd noted that not only were they breaking local by-laws by playing football on the grass but they also had the cheek to use the pole holding up the 'No Ball Games' sign as one of the goalposts. My parents had to go to the cop shop to get him where they were dealt with by a police sergeant who looked at the charge sheet and shook his head in disbelief before releasing my brother and handing him back the ball that the undercovers had confiscated.

Talking of balls, even the balls we played with at school were dangerous as the standard issue was the Mouldmaster, basically an indestructible, solid-hard rubber cannonball with a dimpled surface. If you were stupid enough to header it you were left with at worst brain damage and at the very best a dimpled imprint on your head that lasted for months. It wasn't just responsible for serious head injuries because I've seen really tough gang members cry when it hit them on the bare thigh. I'm talking guys, who would let their Alsatian practise it's vicious biting on their arm without even a murmur, being reduced to tears by the smack of a football. In summer it was painful but bearable, in the winter however, when your legs were cold, the pain was excruciating. This leads me to believe that in pre-anaesthetic times the Mouldmaster was kicked against one leg to take your mind off the surgeon hacking off your other leg with a saw.

The game itself was different, too, in that era as there was none of this modern 'oh hard lines, good shot' appreciation pish you get nowadays for a good try. No, if you shot and missed, no matter if you'd taken the ball from your goalie and dribbled your way past an entire team and overhead volleyed from forty yards out and hit the bar you'd hear, 'You missed ya fucking prick.' Personally I thought that P.E. teachers really shouldn't be using that kind of language but the P.E. teachers I had, Mr Cranston and Mr Ure, were the kind of teachers who did. So much so that they'd write, 'Fucking prick missed a sitter,' on your report card. I might be making that up, but from what I remember they probably did.

Cranston and Ure were typical teachers of the corporal punishment days. In fairness to them they only resorted to corporal punishment because, lobby as they did, the authorities remained very much against their requests to introduce capital punishment as a method of class control in Glasgow schools. Their use of the belt was legendary and on one occasion Ure belted Jim Armour because when we were lined up being given instructions on tactics they asked him a question and he didn't answer. They thought his name was McDonald and, as the question was addressed to a McDonald, Jim was oblivious. After he explained that he didn't answer because he didn't know he was being quizzed, Ure gave him the belt to teach him a lesson for not having the name Ure thought he had.

My school had an incredibly large P.E. department comprising of two indoor games halls, football pitches, two hockey pitches and a running track. It was way bigger than any other department because I'm assuming that the thinking was, 'Well, how much education do they need to pack fags in the Wills Cigarette Factory on Alexandra Parade?' Okay, almost everyone who left at fifteen did indeed end up working there but talk about pigeon-holing.

I was part of the last intake who could leave at fifteen but I didn't and I stayed on. The Education Department had given us a lot of sports facilities but during a visit by a school inspector the P.E. department was criticised for not using them for any sport other than football. Even the hockey pitches were used for a kick about. So one day we all trooped out onto the sports fields and found Thomson and Urquhart standing there not with the usual bibs, usual ball and the usual look of utter contempt on their faces, but with javelins and discuses and the usual look of utter contempt on their faces. This is Easterhouse we're talking about here, an area with horrific gang violence, yet the Education Department deemed it sensible to teach us how to throw spears. Why stop there, what about a few Kalashnikov AK47s, maybe teach us how to drive a fully armed Bren Gun carrier or send us on a two-day course on the correct way to handle a machete when shouting, 'Come intae me, I'll take you all on.'

As for the discus, the only reason I even knew what a discus was was because I'd seen one being thrown in the movie *Jason and the Argonauts*. The movie theme continued when we were all handed a javelin each because we started waving them up and down and chanting, 'Zu . . . lu, zu . . . lu.' Throwing a javelin is fun, for about five minutes. After five minutes, unless you are throwing them at something or, much better still, someone, it's boring. And pointless, because really, how many Olympic javelin throwers have ever come from a Glasgow Scheme? Somehow don't think we'll ever hear, 'And throwing now for Great Britain is Mad Shuggie McNulty from Easterhouse whose previous personal best is managing to hit a moving dog seventy-five yards away.'

The discus is even more boring and there was something

wrong with the discuses anyway because they wouldn't go any more than fifteen feet. The whole pointless exercise lasted about half an hour before the javelins and discuses were gathered in and we went back to football. We actually had a pretty good third-year football team and twice a year we had our grudge match with nearby St Leonards. My school was a Protestant school and St Leonards was a Catholic school so for us it was our Old Firm match. At that point in time religious rivalry was positively encouraged. So much so that at the ABC Minors on Saturday mornings at a cinema in Riddrie, before the big picture, there would be an Old Firm sing song. They'd put song sheets up on the screen with the words of 'It's A Grand Old Team To Play For' for the Catholic kids and then 'Follow Follow We Will Follow Rangers' for the Protestant kids and the compere would come on stage with a pointer to highlight the words while challenging us to out-sing each other. In today's completely over-legislated climate, he'd be up in court on a charge of inciting sectarian hatred.

Large crowds always gathered to watch the Westwood vs St Leonards matches, usually comprising of drunk men who only seemed to be there to shout, 'Get intae these Proddy bastards,' or, 'Get intae these Fenian bastards,' at fifteen-year-olds, or if they could get their drunken acts together they managed a few verses of 'The Sash' or 'The Soldier's Song'. I say managed a few verses but since neither of them knew the words past about half way through the second verses, there was a lot of mumbling and dee dee dees from that point on. On the upside, the bigoted abuse was balanced out to both sides, which I thought was quite fair-minded.

But there was one time I did hear something that made absolutely no sense. At half time we were given the obligatory half time quarter of an orange and one man who was more mental than most started shouting, 'Oranges, aw that's just fucking typical.' An orange is a fruit, not a symbol of the Protestant faith. You do get King Edward potatoes, but you don't get King Billy oranges. He obviously thought you did and the half time orange was part of a huge conspiracy by citrus fruit growers to subliminally support Protestantism.

The abusers would even be wearing Rangers or Celtic scarves and tammies, the only attire available at the time to show team allegiance. Football tops were only available to the players because it was long before Rangers and Celtic came up with the idea to make money from selling items of clothing which a) would make them a lot of money, and b) make their fans stand out and give them more of a chance to get themselves beaten up. Why anyone in Glasgow, which is a dangerous enough place, would want to wear a top that increases the dangers tenfold is completely beyond me. Many years later I'd arranged to play five-a-sides with Dominik Diamond, easily Scotland's greatest DJ and talk radio host. Not only is Dominik both of these things, he's also one of Scotland's most famous professional Celtic fans. As I hadn't played football in years I didn't have a top so I went out and bought a generic one that wasn't the strip of any team, the reason being that I didn't want to show my allegiance to any club on health and safety grounds. It's not healthy or safe to cut about in Glasgow in an Old Firm top.

As the five-a-sides were within walking distance of our houses, Dominik arranged to come and get me and we'd walk up together. He duly arrived in a Celtic away top. I asked him, 'Are you mental?' He was always complaining of getting hassled by Rangers fans because he just can't keep his yapper shut when it comes to criticism of Rangers and its fans, and being six-foot-two with a distinctive goatee beard doesn't exactly help him blend into the background either. And he blends in even less in a Celtic away top. So we walked to the pitches and he did get hassle but I didn't hear what the hassle was because I made him and his Celtic away top walk a hundred yards in front of me.

In my opinion football jerseys are work clothing. Would people put on a Celtic top and hang around outside the City

Chambers? Mind you if the rumours that Glasgow Council only ever employs Catholics are true then perhaps a Celtic top is the Glasgow Council staff uniform. The point is, do they think people will look at them, see a middle-aged man with a beer gut and say to themselves, 'Hey look, he's wearing a Rangers top, he must be one of the players.' No, people look at them and think, 'Aw look at that poor man, he thinks he's a four-year-old.' Kids wearing tops is fine, because kids are daft. They wear policeman and fireman outfits and footballers tops because when they grow up they want to be them, and they still might be. But when you're forty-five you've grown up not to be a footballer so let it go, your life is what it's become and you aren't fooling anyone apart from yourself.

In the pre-sportswear decades you only wore sportswear if you could afford sportswear for sports. Now 99% of it is worn by people who not only look like they don't do sport they look as though they've got absolutely no idea what sport is. I could be wrong though and maybe walking about Braehead shopping mall overweight and sweating while carrying more new sportswear that you won't wear for sport in a Sports Division bag is indeed a sport. If it is a sport then I take back what I said and it's nice to see so many Scots training in the hope of winning a gold medal for Fatty and Sweatyathalon at the Glasgow Commonwealth Games in 2014.

As for baseball caps, the police should arrest everyone they see wearing one because if they aren't on their way to committing a crime they are on their way back from carrying one out. Here's a question: what's more suspicious-looking in Glasgow than someone in sportswear running? What's more suspicious in Glasgow is someone in sportswear tiptoeing. And for God's sake don't get an Old Firm tattoo. Don't, just don't. Having a Red Hand of Ulster or an 1888 Shamrock on your forehead is going to look pretty stupid when you're seventy and down at the post office picking up your pension. Even more stupid than it looks now. Tattoos? I know a guy who's got 1690 on one cheek, a union jack on the other cheek, a Red Hand on his neck and Rangers written down his nose. I asked him why his forehead was blank and he told me, 'I was going to get Rangers Champions League Winners 2011/2012 on my forehead, but I wouldn't want to get something I might regret in later life.' That didn't happen, I'm just illustrating the point.

And what about that poor guy who got Ally McCoist's name on his leg and the tattoo artist spelt it Ally McOist. What did he learn from this? He learned from this that the tattoo artist he went to was a Celtic fan.

I digress. I wish I could remember how the matches against St Leonards finished but I can't because the police were always called and the game became less about what was happening on the park and more about what was happening around it. You do tend to lose count of the score when there's the hilarious distraction of grown men who really should know better being bundled into a Black Maria.

Not wanting to blow my own trumpet, but I was a pretty good player, I was a right-footed left winger to be exact. I played for my school, for the Boys Brigade and a local team called Lochbridge, and it was during a Lochbridge match that I was spotted by a talent scout from Celtic Boys Club, probably the best youth team in Scotland at that time. After a trial, I joined them and that's when my problems really started. We trained Monday and Wednesday nights at Celtic's training ground in Barrowfield near Parkhead. This might sound like a so what. Well the so what was that Celtic Boys Club had a dress code which meant I had to wear a green blazer with the Celtic badge on, tie and grey flannels, and I had to carry a Celtic bag. So my routine was leaving my house in Wardie Road, getting chased to the bus stop 800 yards away on Edinburgh Road, being verbally abused at the bus stop, verbally abused on the bus, and after getting off the bus being chased another 800 yards from Parkhead Cross to Barrowfield – a process that worked in reverse on the journey home. This might sound like an exaggeration but it isn't.

As for Barrowfield – as God forsaken places go, God had forsaken it. Barrowfield was said to be worse than Beirut, and this was said by the people of Beirut. Even the police were afraid to enter the area. No one in Barrowfield had any electrical appliances because Hutchinson's and Stepek refused to deliver anywhere near the place. And I had to go through this area twice a week and once at weekends if we had a home match. Ah yes, but Celtic's training ground at Barrowfield had two pitches, one of which was grass and playing on grass made up for about 5% of what I had to go through to get there.

When you are fifteen, things don't occur to you. Things like, why are some of the coaches taking the Catholic players to the pictures and not inviting me and the three other Protestant players in the team. Not that we were in the least bothered because none of us really fancied seeing *The Sound of Music*, like not fancied seeing it ever, ever. But there were other things too, weird things, but why I thought they were weird I just couldn't put my finger on. For instance, being told that we couldn't wear our underpants underneath our nylon shorts. This I ignored because we're talking the seventies and the shorts were so thin that without the warmth of a pair of underpants your testicles would end up looking like the two tiny wee grapes that every bunch of grapes has, the two tiny wee grapes that for some reason haven't grown like the others. Plus seventies shorts were so tiny you looked like a rent boy.

As it transpired, that was the last thing you wanted to look like at Celtic Boys Club. Also some coaches wanted to rub wintergreen on your legs in the winter to keep your muscles warm. An offer I always declined by saying, 'Cold, naw, it's phew, pure boiling out there.' I didn't at the time know why but I never stayed for a shower after a match. I'd just get my clothes on and go. It was many, many years later when the news broke about what it was that I couldn't put my finger on. I couldn't put my finger on it, but one of the coaches did put his finger on it, many times, and that was the reason he ended up in jail. My first reaction to the news was, well that certainly explains a lot, and my second reaction was, thank God my Protestant upbringing forbade me from ever asking to see *The Sound of Music*.

I do remember passing a cinema in Sauchiehall Street when *The Sound of Music* first hit the screens and the queue seemed to comprise entirely of Nuns waiting to get in. This led to me thinking to myself that the Little Sisters of the Poor can't be that poor if they can afford cinema tickets, popcorn and a hot dog. To this day I still haven't seen *The Sound of Music* and all I know about it is that it's got something to do with a nun, a Nazi and the BBC broadcasting a very long series of adverts for Andrew Lloyd Webber's West End production of it.

When what had been going on under my nose at Celtic Boys Club was revealed I was working on the TV show *Only An Excuse*, and being a comedy writer I thought why not write a sketch about it, which I did. Admittedly not the funniest theme for a sketch, but it wasn't really about that, sort of . . .

The sketch was Johnny Watson in silhouette with the Celtic Boys Club crest in the background and it was Johnny saying, 'What happened was I was sitting in the dressing room and, and [sobbing] no I'm alright . . . and the manager came into the dressing room and he sat down beside me [sobbing], sorry this is really hard for me [sobbing] . . . and he put his arm around me and hold on, give me a minute to compose myself, it was horrible so it was, sorry, right I'm okay. So he sat down beside me and put his arm around me and he . . . and he . . . and he . . . and he told me he was dropping me for Peter Grant.'

After much discussion between the show's producer Phil Differ and worried BBC executives, Phil persuaded them to broadcast the sketch, and if you saw it and laughed at it, shame on you. But really, could you imagine actually being dropped for Peter Grant. You'd just never get over that would you?

All this aside, we did have a brilliant team who remained unbeaten during my time with them. We weren't just unbeaten, we defeated every team we came across by a huge margin, and I played in every match, bar one. The one match I didn't play in was against St Mary's Borstal in Bishopbriggs. When we arrived it was snowing and cold. The snow and the cold I could deal with because I had my warm underpants on, but then I saw the St Mary's Borstal team, probably the scariest looking mob I'd ever seen. That ugly scary thing some people have. You know when you go into a pub and you notice someone and you just know by their face that they are going to assault someone at some point in the night by either asking, 'Whit you looking at?' or, 'Hey, are you looking at ma burd?' or, 'How come you're no looking at ma burd?' Well the entire team comprised of hims. Added to that, two of the inmates had the sticks with nails on that are used to prod holes in the ground to drain water away from the goal mouth and they were throwing them and trying to stick them in the cross bar above our goalies head during the warm up.

So, I think the phrase here is 'I shat it' and feigned the flu. I was only half believed and despite my very serious flu-like symptoms, which I'm pretty sure could have progressed into made-up double pneumonia, I was made a sub. I assumed that, given their violent appearance, one of our outfield players would be off injured within thirty seconds and I'd be sent on to die, or I'd end up in goals while our keeper is ambulanced off to the Royal Infirmary to have a stick with a nail in it surgically removed from the back of his head. But I was really lucky because the snow starting falling so heavily that the game had to be abandoned after fifteen minutes.

On a historical note, I was playing for Celtic against a Doctor Barnardo's Homes team on 23 October 1971, the day Celtic and Partick Thistle contested the League Cup Final. My dad, who was a Thistle fan, knew Thistle were going to win, claiming divine intervention by the Godlike Japanese Emperor Hirohito. Let me explain what my dad explained. Emperor Hirohito had only been in Britain on one previous occasion, which had been in 1921, and when he was here Thistle beat Rangers 1-0 in the

Scottish Cup Final. The Emperor was visiting Britain again fifty years on and Thistle were in the League Cup final, therefore Thistle would win. And they did, which makes: 'Why should Partick Thistle thank Emperor Hirohito?' the ultimate pub quiz question. One of those 'I'll bet you a million pounds you'll never get this' posers. You will now, obviously because I've just told you about it.

At half time in my match the news filtered through that Celtic were 4-0 down going into the break. As Celtic were at their peak at the time everyone assumed that the radio announcer had made a mistake and Celtic were 4-0 up. When the truth became known the other three Rangers fans in the team and myself almost broke our faces trying not to grin, and we couldn't speak either because there was no way we'd be able to say anything that didn't sound like a gloat.

I eventually left Celtic Boys Club for a few reasons. On one particular Saturday I'd played early in the morning for the Boys Brigade, and mid-morning I played for the school and in the afternoon match with Celtic Boys Club I went down with cramp in the second half. As all the Celtic players were super fit, cramp shouldn't have been an issue but as I was on my third game that day, plus having been chased to the bus and then chased to Barrowfield, it was. I was told I would have to give up my other teams, something I just wasn't really prepared to do.

That was one reason, the other was that we had a Saturday off because we had a cup final on the Sunday and they wanted the team to stand in Glasgow City Centre in their blazers collecting money for Scottish youth teams or some other such charity, if it even existed. I think my actual words were, 'Aye, that'll be right.' This was met with me being told, 'If you don't turn up on Saturday, don't bother turning up on Sunday.' I didn't turn up on the Saturday, ergo. On Sunday they won without me and I thought that was the end of it. But the coach came to my door on the Monday night asking me to come back but I refused because I just couldn't be arsed with all the hassle and the getting kicked up and down the park during every match. My dad was pretty angry because he envisaged a career in football for me but I had other plans and I really wanted to train as the rear gunner on the late night bus to Castlemilk.

My mother was glad though because we weren't the richest family in the world and keeping me kitted out was expensive. My boots were Puma and they cost £7, which then was about a quarter of my dad's weekly wage, then there was the blazer and flannels, etc, even more expense, and not forgetting the studs which had to be replaced frequently. Nowadays you can get all that stuff at Primark for about £3, or for nothing if you wait for the Primark sale.

The only upside of my time at Celtic Boys Club was when I met Jock Stein and he spoke to me. The Celtic ground staff were on strike and as the club had an important European tie the youth teams were drafted in to clean up the stadium. And do you know what Jock Stein said to me? He said something that I will never forget. He said, 'Naw son, that's not how you work a brush, come get yer back intae it.' It was a very proud moment. Celtic didn't pay us, the strike breaking scabs that we were, instead they gave each of us a packet of Golden Wonder crisps and a jubilee. Perhaps Celtic paid their ground staff in crisps and jubilees too and that's why they were on strike. I wish now that I'd kept the crisps and the jubilee because I'm sure some daftie would, given their provenance, pay a fortune for them on eBay. There are those who claim that Big Jock knew what was happening at the Boys Club but in all honesty I doubt it.

Once or twice my mates and I played rounders but we found out that unless you were throwing the ball or trying to hit it, the standing around on the off chance it would come in your direction was pretty boring. Another sport we played was tennis but that was only ever during Wimbledon because that was the only time the staff in Blairtummock Park could be arsed opening its two fenced-in tennis courts. For about 10p you could hire a racket and a ball. A ball, singular, so you couldn't do the putting the spare balls in your trouser pockets and make 'hey look, I've got giant testicles' jokes. The ball itself that you got to hire for your 10p was so old it didn't even bounce and would land with a dull thud and practically stop dead. It was so lifeless that the only way you could get a rally going was to get within three feet of the net and keep it in the air by hitting it underhand at each other. The rackets, too, could have done with being restrung because you shouldn't have been able to get the ball stuck in the strings. Still it was nice of the Fred Perry Museum to donate his old 1930's wooden rackets to the council.

The courts didn't even have proper chalked markings because that probably meant having to re-mark the courts every couple of days. Instead they laid plastic strip markings and nailed them down, and they weren't even nailed down properly because after about five minutes of playing they'd rise up a few inches and you'd end up tripping over them. The nets fared a bit better as they were indeed the regulation three foot six, but only at both ends because they drooped down to a non-regulation nine inches or so in the middle. The fat kids thought this was great because it let them jump over the net if they won. And this was all, of course, if you could play tennis at all. I went for a game with a mate once and the park attendant told us we we'd have to share a racket because someone had stolen the other one. The theft came as a bit of a shock to us because how could anyone manage to sneak a racket past the incredibly tight security of the man sitting in a small hut next to the courts reading a paper. The bigger question was, however, how exactly do you share a racket. It's no wonder therefore that Scotland doesn't produce that many tennis players, but it does explain why Andy Murray is so good. It's because he never had to share a racket in council tennis courts in Glasgow.

Admittedly there was a bowling green next to the tennis courts but really, come on, bowls isn't a sport. It's just something old people do while they are waiting to die.

When my family eventually left Easterhouse for East Kilbride my dad joined the Red Deer Bowling Club in Westwood (no relation to my school) and they competed every year with other East Kilbride bowling clubs for a trophy sponsored by the Co-operative Funeral Society. So, bowls, old people waiting to die, definitely. I think winning the cup entitled the victors to a 10% discount on a funeral. Every September the Co-op would give the bowling clubs leaflets warning, 'Book your funeral now to avoid the winter rush.'

When my Father passed away his entire bowling club descended on the funeral meal like locusts and ate everything. One even had the cheek to tell me that we'd run out of sandwiches. Well, maybe if just a couple of you had come to represent the whole club instead of two busloads of you greedy bastards turning up then there would have been enough food to go round. But no, a big day out for them, obviously.

If you are planning a funeral for a loved one who's a member of a bowling club, have the funeral in the late afternoon because even free food can't compete with *Countdown*. Incidentally, we didn't use the Co-op Funeral Society for my dad's funeral as I thought that them sponsoring a bowls tournament was not only a wee bit cheeky but a big bit ghoulish.

11

SOCKS AND DUGS AND ROCK'N'ROLL

Third year at school was the year of division. Those who were leaving, namely Jacko and Eddie, formed a different pack and would while away the days either dogging it or smoking behind the games hall. They decided that they were now adults and would soon be going out into the world to make their way, the rest of us were still kids with, in some cases, three years still to go.

I was staying on, as I wanted qualifications in the hope of avoiding a manual job. I had seen the workmen building the new school extension in mid-winter and thought bugger that. The men were blue with cold with their breath turning to frost as they swore when their hands were too numb to get their thermos flasks open for some hot soup.

No, I wanted a cushy job. In fact my only ambition was to make the most amount of money for the least amount of work, but then again, isn't that everyone's?

Only Winker, Wilco and myself in our crowd were staying on. Nearly three quarters intended leaving as soon as they legally could. It was quite sad really as a lot of them had brains but the call of the overall in the Wills Cigarette Factory was just too strong. Everyone who left at fifteen ended up there, drawn by not only good wages but the monthly allocation of free fags as well. We settled down to our studies with a new vigour and for the first time we actually listened to what the teacher had to say. The teachers, however, viewed this with great suspicion.

Mr Brown, our woodwork teacher, was by far the most

suspicious. He became so nervous of our intentions that he'd check that we hadn't sawn through a leg of his chair before he sat down.

About two weeks into the term he entered the class and found Winker with the class Ug's – Bugsy Millar's – head locked in the vice and thumping him with a piece of four-by-two. Winker had caught Bugsy looking at his willie in the shower after P.E. and took exception to it. Mr Brown belted Winker but the relief on the teacher's face was evident and it was obvious he was glad to see the class returning to normal.

In English we started to do Shakespeare, which was met with an attitude approaching hostility. All the thys, thous and ancient dialect was beyond our comprehension and we just recited it parrot fashion, unsure of what exactly was coming out of our mouths.

Our English teacher was a good-looking woman in her mid-thirties, Mrs Cairney, and she had this habit of sitting on her desk with her feet on the chair in front of her. From every angle you could see up her skirt. Winker and myself were always stuck in the front row and got more of a view than anyone else.

One day Winker turned to me and said, 'Christ ye can almost taste it can't ye?'

Fortunately, she never heard that comment but when she asked Winker to read something off the board, he replied, 'Well maybe if ye moved yer fanny out of the way I could see the board.' It was plain for all to see that she'd heard that one. Winker was stunned. He hadn't actually thought that his mouth would say what his brain was thinking but it did. The class sat in shocked silence. Winker was dragged out of his seat and along to the headmaster's office where he was given twelve of the belt and suspended for two weeks.

When he was allowed to return to the class we were about to do *Hamlet* and Mrs Cairney had a special treat in store for Winker.

He was given the part of Osric the Fop. She went on in great detail explaining exactly what a fop was, which was basically a Shakespearean big Jessie. Sort of a cross between Scotland's celebrity big jessies Colin and Justin. This only resulted in Winker dogging English for a further fortnight to avoid being labelled a Jessie for the rest of his school life.

I was given the part and I suffered.

After two weeks Winker returned, figuring he was now safe as the die had been cast. Wrong. He was given the part the moment he popped his head round the classroom door. For about a month everyone called him Larry Grayson and every time he entered a classroom there would be a shout of 'shut that door'. Winker did take it in good humour, mainly because he had to because he couldn't have battered everyone. To do so he'd have had to batter at night and batter double time at weekends just to keep on top of things.

Around this time we gained a new addition to our crowd. Big Ally Dixon, a tall blond kid who wouldn't have looked out of place in the Hitler Youth. He was a very brash and abrasive character who had knowledge far beyond his years. He joined Winker, Wilco and I, and the four of us became the school pupils committee for our year whereby we were allowed to take teachers to task over any grievances, real or imaginary, we may have.

One of the major moans was the school never took us on trips anymore.

Not since Hush Hush had we engaged in any extracurricular activities, so after a lot of argy bargy it was decided that a trip to the theatre wouldn't bankrupt the school funds. We didn't decide the theatre, the teachers did, because the education department had a list of trips they'd fund and as the list only comprised of theatres or museums, the theatre was chosen because it was top of the list of two.

Unfortunately the trip coincided with our curiosity with alcohol and we decided to visit a pub before we went on down to the theatre. We arranged to meet in the Stevedore and Taylors pub at the top of Buchanan Street (sadly no longer there, they should have put up a plaque saying 99% of under Glaswegian under-agers had their first drink on this site).

I arrived first in my new three-piece suit looking as much an eighteen-year-old as a fifteen-year-old can possibly look. To my astonishment the barman asked me what I wanted and not being too well versed in the arts of ordering a drink, I said, 'A drink of beer please.'

'What dae ye mean a drink of beer – a pint or half pint?'

'A *pint.*'

'A pint of what pal?'

'Guinness.'

I got my pint of Guinness and sat down, it tasted vile and the only reason I had asked for Guinness was because I'd heard the comedian Dave Allen talking about it on the telly. I sat with it feeling very ill at ease but trying to look as though I had been in pubs all my life. The other three came in, Big Ally went up to the bar and ordered, he was also served and brought the drinks over.

He looked at my pint of Guinness and said, 'That's a fucking Tim's drink.'

He took a sip from his own glass containing lager and went off to the toilet.

We sat and surveyed the surroundings, the place was full of wee Jimmys with gruff woodbine voices who spoke in some strange dialect we couldn't understand. I later found out that this is the common language of those in the advanced stages of alcohol abuse. We should maybe have guessed how advanced their alcoholic abuse was when they waved money at us saying, 'I'll gie ye a fiver fur yer liver.'

Big Ally returned from the toilet and said he'd been in this pub a hundred times before and therefore he was a regular. We sat in awe as he criticised the staff, the decor and the fruit machine, which he referred to as a 'rip off'. He went up to the bar and returned with a brandy and a cigar then sat back down looking a bit like a gangster in an old black and white movie.

'No bad brandy this, it's Napoleonic.'

He took a drink and then a large puff on his cigar. It looked really cool until he choked and spat his drink all over Winker and Wilco's faces.

'Aw jeez oh man.'

The whole bar turned round to look at us and there we were, four fifteen-year-olds, two looking embarrassed and the other two looking wet.

We drank up and left.

We met the rest of the class down at the Citz – the Citizen's Theatre. We had two teachers supervising us and they gave us the rules, stay together, stay out of the bar and stay out of trouble.

Ally said that the teachers could go fuck themselves and asked me if I was coming to the bar for a drink at half time. I think it's called the interval in the theatre, I told him.

'Well are you coming to the bar in the interval then, Laurence fucking Olivier?'

'We'll see.'

But after watching a very actor-y pish play about the Americanisation of Japan in which the lead character said 'Gee Dolores' all the time, I was ready for any diversion at the interval.

'Mon, we'll hide in the corner, no one will see us.'

He only had enough money left for one brandy, so there we were, Ally with his brandy and smoking a cigarette, and Wilco and Winker outside looking in through glass panels in the wall.

Ally must have had a very weak bladder because he asked to me to hold his drink and his fag as he was going off for a 'desperately needed pish' as he put it. Stupidly I took his accoutrements and was standing with them when the teacher walked in.

He saw me and came straight over.

'What the bloody hell do you think you are doing?'

I started to stutter but denials were useless as I had the

evidence in my hand. Ally came back in, clocked the scene and got off his mark.

I reported to the teacher next day and got six of the belt.

A month after this I had my first real drink. It was someone's sixteenth birthday party in Blairtummock House, the large mansion in the public park. It was the only thing remaining from the family who had once owned the land Easterhouse was built on before they'd wisely sold up and moved on. It was now hired out by the council for functions and we were all invited to attend on the Saturday night.

Big Ally said he would arrange the bevy so pre-party we went up to his house for a wee swally. When he said he would arrange the swally we thought he meant a can of lager, but no, his father worked in a whisky bond and periodically he would drain the sediment from the bottom of the vats and take it home with him.

On its own, the sediment tasted vile but diluted with cream soda it was very palatable indeed, so palatable that you couldn't even taste the alcohol and I like to think that we'd just invented the first ever alcopop. You're welcome. At that age you have no concept whatsoever of the effects of alcohol and there we were knocking back pints of the stuff.

At first we felt great, absolutely great, the world was ours and everyone was our friend.

We left Ally's house and staggered the 400 yards or so to the party and made our big entrance. We had arrived 'nae bother to us by the way'.

I spied the school captain sitting next to a girl. I shuffled over and in my alcoholic inhibition, said to him, 'I think you're a fucking prick.'

Statement made, I then collapsed on the floor and started, for the want of a better phrase, puking my load. I dragged myself off to the toilet and just lay there with my head down the pan. One by one Ally, Winker and Wilco appeared and did the same thing. We lay there for three hours unable to move. I asked God many times to let me die but he obviously wasn't listening. We were all wretching violently and anyone who entered the toilets could see our backsides in a formation puking team sort of a thing. We should have been hospitalised because we definitely had alcohol poisoning.

We couldn't move and lay there semi-comatose. We were getting a lot of verbal abuse and kicks up the arse for hogging the toilets and at one point someone came into my cubicle and pissed over my head. I like to think he was aiming for the pan but in retrospect he probably did mean to piss on me as I was pissing him off.

The party ended at ten o'clock and we had to leave but couldn't stand unaided. We were gathered up by those more sober than we were and taken along to another party. I had my arms over two guys shoulders and my feet were getting dragged along behind me. On the way there I lost a shoe. We reached the other venue and it was a smarty party, i.e. no drink and just sweeties and ginger. For east coast readers, ginger is a generic term on the west coast for a soft drink.

I was hauled into the living room and deposited in front of the TV where I collapsed in a heap, much to the annoyance of the host's father who was trying to watch *Scotsport*. Drunk and dying though I was I still managed a snigger when I heard an Arthur Montfordism. He said, 'The Celtic fans came expecting steak and went away with mince.' Not up there with 'what a stramash', but still brilliant nonetheless.

I was lying there so ill that I couldn't even sit up for appearances sake, I just lay there whimpering, limp and with one shoe missing.

Eventually we came round enough to walk to Ally's house, albeit with the aid of fences, parked cars and each other. We went into his bedroom and collapsed and lay there fully clothed and covered in and stinking of vomit. Winker managed the strength to say, 'See as soon as I feel better Dixon I'm gonnie kick your head right in ya tube.'

Ally didn't answer him as he was too ill.

Thankfully I ended up in the arms of Morpheus and I awoke next morning very surprised as I was sure I would have passed away in my sleep. One by one the other three awoke. Winker was claiming that he was blind in one eye, Wilco with a face so translucent you could see his skull through his skin, and Ally none the worse for wear. It was at this point that we decided we hated him. Him and his hair that was too blond even for the Third Reich.

After a lot of moaning and groaning we decided to head home to recuperate and the three of us started what seemed like an endless trek homeward. The sun was splitting the trees and the light was boring into our eyes like a Black & Decker drill. I was hobbling as I had lost one shoe and I had sick in my hair but I was far too ill to care. We split up and went up our own streets.

I passed my mother who was on her way to church with her friends, she looked at me, declined to comment and kept on walking. I got home and slid into bed. It felt great to get under the covers but no sooner had my head hit the pillow than my father started to hoover the house and stick a Sydney Devine record on the old Dansette. At that point I reached the lowest ebb in my life.

Incidentally, it was another four years before I really touched drink ever again, even the smell of lager was enough to bring the sorry scene back and make me vomit. Ironically, every time I put on my records my dad would bang on the bedroom door and tell me to turn the music down because it was annoying the neighbours. Yes, but he had no problem with Sydney Devine at full blast annoying the neighbours. He had no problem with that. No problem at all. My father didn't like my music and although I was allowed to watch *Top of the Pops* I couldn't hear it half the time for his criticisms of the acts. 'Look at their hair, you can't even tell if it's a man or woman.' That was one of his favourites. Another was, 'Bloody noise,' and yet another, 'You can't even hear a word they are singing.'

If he did like a song he was full of praise, but it was always for songs that I hated. The phrase he used when he actually liked something was 'bags of rhythm'. He'd say, 'I like Lieutenant Pigeon's "Mouldy Old Dough", it's got bags of rhythm.' He did say once that he didn't know why Sydney Devine never made it onto *Top of the Pops*. I would have explained, but I never swore in front of my parents.

I returned to school on the Monday still feeling God awful but we were cheered by the news that the school had been given a grant to buy musical instruments. The money was intended for cellos and flutes and the likes but after a Teacher/Pupil discussion we persuaded them to release the funds for guitars and drums. After our first musical foray, which ended abruptly, we were going to get another chance.

The whole school wanted to be pop stars and have access to the equipment but after a lot of threatening behaviour from Winker and Ally we got exclusive third-year access. The fourth-year boys also started a band and we rehearsed on alternative days. We had slightly more musical knowledge than they did though and they soon got bored with it and left us with total access.

To justify the expenditure we would have to play the school dance and the Headie came up with a list of songs he thought it would be nice if we could learn. Winker took one look at the list, saw 'Beautiful Sunday', and ripped it up. We remembered the fiasco of the first school band's appearance and decided that we would have to be much, much better than them. We wanted people cheering and shouting how great we were, not jeering at how shite we were.

The equipment was top of the range so at least if we weren't exactly brilliant we would sound good even if we were bad. We now had a different line up: Winker on vocals, Ally on drums, Kenny on lead guitar, me on bass and this bloke Ronnie that no one liked except Kenny on rhythm. Since Kenny was the best amongst us and we needed him, we had to go along with his

Ronnie decision. One big problem we did have was deciding what we'd play. Everyone liked different things. Kenny liked Queen but Winker told him in no uncertain terms that he wasn't going to sing any Queen songs because Freddie Mercury had 'big giant buck teeth' as he so eloquently put it. By that I think he meant that he couldn't identify with him, and not being able to identify with a singer was also the reason he wouldn't sing any songs sung by 'daft burds either' as he again so eloquently put it. Kenny did at one point say we should write our own songs, but that was shouted down because the one thing an audience doesn't ever want to hear is 'and here's one we wrote ourselves' unless it's said by the Beatles. Plus most lyrics are pretty bad or don't really make much sense and whatever we did write would have been in both categories. The worst of the former category for me was a UFO song which began with the line, 'She was a Brownie, I was a Scout, she showed me how to shake it about,' and the latter, despite being a classic, is Free's 'Alright Now': 'There she stood in the street, smiling from her head to her feet.' So basically she's just one giant head with feet growing out of her chin? Somehow I don't think so Paul Rodgers, Andy Fraser, Simon Kirke and Paul Kossoff.

On the playing front, I was only ever an adequate bass player and I learned to play by numbers. In other words, two plucks of G, then a B, A, then back to G. I once spent an entire weekend learning to play Cream's 'Sunshine of Your Love' exactly as it sounded on the record and when the band came to learning it Kenny said, 'Okay, we'll do it in the key of G.' My answer to that was, 'Unless G is what I've learned it in then no we fucking won't.'

We rehearsed most days and became quite proficient. The only problem we encountered, apart from Winker's ego, was volume. We'd start off balanced and you could hear every instrument clearly then someone would decide that their guitar was too low and turn it up. This led to someone else turning theirs up and so on. Pretty soon all you could hear would be Winker screaming above the feedback.

SOCKS AND DUGS AND ROCK'N'ROLL

And, of course, we needed a name. For some reason Winker decided that he was the band and we were his backing group and he thought the name Winker's Blues Warriors was quite apt. No one agreed with him.

'Oh aye fuckin' Popeye, why stop there? Why not Winker and his Wankers?'

It was settled democratically when Ronnie beat Winker up and we simply became the Blues Warriors. But only after a teacher explained to us why we couldn't use our first choice of Master Bass. Apparently it sounded an awful lot like another word.

We were to play for the first years to kick off the dance season, and as the night of the gig approached our confidence ebbed and we started crapping ourselves. We sat backstage and listened to the usual Heelan' records come to a close and the Headie giving his usual speech.

He said will you now welcome the Westwood School group, the . . . the . . . he went into his pocket for the piece of paper with our name on it and eventually got it right. The curtain went back. Before we took the stage Ronnie went off to the toilet and we'd forgotten to tell him we'd decided to open with Alex Harvey's 'Midnight Moses' instead of Deep Purple's 'Strange Kind Of Woman'.

The result was chaos. He was playing one thing and we were all playing another. For some reason he blamed Winker for this and called him a stupid fucker. We composed ourselves and started again. This time we were all in tune with one another and surprised ourselves so much that we all had broad grins on our faces, which was hardly the mean moody look we were going for but we couldn't help ourselves as we were on a roll. After a few numbers the crowd actually started to dance and, at the end of a song, went into wild applause.

We finished the set and left the stage.

They were screaming for an encore, we went back out but as we had exhausted our full repertoire of four songs we had to repeat a couple of the songs. They didn't care. We finished and walked off after Ally had walked to the front of the stage and thrown his drumsticks into the melee and they started fighting over them.

This was glory, this was fame and we went backstage and started congratulating ourselves until Ronnie, who was strangely silent throughout all the backslapping, said, 'Well whit did ye expect, anything's better than they fuckin' ballroom records and they even mair fuckin' Heelan' records. That lot would have asked for an encore if I had farted.'

He was always capable of putting a dampener on things.

Ally was well pissed off with him and a few weeks later murdered his budgie 'Tottie' in a revenge attack. Not really murdered as such. We were in Ronnie's living room with our guitars and while Ronnie had gone to the toilet, Ally took a shot of it and turned the volume up to full, strummed it and the noise gave the budgie a heart attack and it landed with a very small thump in the bottom of its cage. When Ronnie came back from the toilet he went mental because not only was his budgie dead, but the man who lived below him was on the nightshift and he'd get a telling off when the man told his mum about the racket.

12

LEAD ON MACDUFF

After the Christmas break we returned to school for what was going to be most of the class's last term. Those of us staying did our best to learn but the leavers had no intention of spending their last five months in any sort of educational pursuits and the classes were disrupted at every opportunity.

One by one the leavers played truant, then disappeared entirely.

This left the rest of us to ponder the advantages of a long-term education. Fifteen is an awkward age, money or lack of it had become important and in a few months time our classmates were going to become wage earners whilst the supposedly brainier lot wouldn't see any real cash for another three years.

It was a tough choice to stay or leave but my parents had attended one of the parent's nights and were told that I had a chance, so from then on I had no choice. I was staying on for the duration and that was that. I said I could leave after the O-levels and get a job then but no, I was ordered by my dad to get Highers as well, and if you knew my dad you'd have got higher too.

The lessons at times seemed inane and pointless but I felt I had to learn something for my parents' sake. We were not a rich family and as they were going to have to fund me for a further two, maybe three years, I'd have to give them some gold at the end of their rainbow.

It was a strange changeover. Once the teachers had learned that we were willing to listen a bit, their attitudes altered. We still had a mischievous streak but they were now more apt to view our 'getting through the day' with more humour than we thought was possible.

Our Geography teacher that year was a Mr Johnstone and he looked every inch like a Geography teacher. He had glasses, cords, tweed jacket, beard and thick walking shoes. Come to think of it he looked every inch like Gerry Adams. His classes were fun. If we asked stupid questions we got stupid answers. But sometimes our questions weren't so much questions as attempts to get him to sound as though he was swearing.

We'd heard about Shi-ite Muslims on the news and so we asked him, 'What's a shi-ite surr, know a shi-ite surr, what is that, the shi-ite thing surr, know?' Patiently he explained and managed not even once to not sound like he was saying Shi-ite.

He had a way of handling the class that we'd never come across before. If we didn't want to learn we were to sit at the back of the class and amuse ourselves and if we did want to learn we were to sit at the front and listen.

Also, on entering his class Winker and myself were ordered out to the front.

'Any jokes, comments or remarks before we start?'

'Em . . . no, Sir.'

'Great, now sit down.'

It worked and we very seldom misbehaved. His classes were interesting probably because he didn't teach us normal geography and would basically just tell us of his travels and strange encounters he had experienced. We loved it and I'm sure he had a soft spot for us.

He was also the only teacher who caught me red-handed and never belted me. One Friday afternoon he left the room to go to the toilet and while he was away I was hit on the back of the head with a rubber thrown by Crammond, a really irksome kid who had one of those faces you just want to slap. I jumped out of my seat, grabbed Crammond's bag and swung it above my head. I had started the swing when Johnstone walked back in and it was too late to stop. Crammond, seeing the teacher enter, thought he was safe and stupidly clasped his hands on the desk in innocence instead of using them to protect himself. The bag almost dislocated his head from his shoulders.

Johnstone asked me to the front of the class.

'It's Friday and there's only five minutes to go before you and I commence our weekend, and now I have caught you assaulting another pupil. Maybe Mr Crammond deserved it, I don't know, so I am going to flip a coin, heads I belt you, tails I don't.'

He then flicked up a ten pence and I guessed heads.

'Very lucky, return to your seat.'

I could have sworn I saw a tail. In the seventies we were taught that the world was heading for a new ice age. In fact we were taught that a lot because scientists had confirmed this, so therefore it was true. In the new millennium that very same science has changed its mind and the biggie now is global warming, which is apparently worse than they first predicted. The problem is that they predicted that it was going to destroy the planet, and what's worse than that? Just destroying part of the planet but leaving Paisley intact. At least in the seventies anyone who didn't buy into the ice age scenario wasn't thought of as some kind of heretic because everyone was allowed to have an opinion. However, not believing that man is responsible for global warming has now become heresy. Even though the environmentalists have moved the goalposts somewhat and now refer to it as climate change because people who spend the winter up to their arses in snow were starting to doubt the global warming theory. Despite what we were taught as gospel, the new ice age never happened and all that work we did in Geography compiling graphs to indicate which crops would fail first when the temperature fell, and drawing maps showing Scotland as one big glacier, were a complete waste time. No matter how much a waste of time, it was still time much better spent than on algebra.

Our attitudes changed towards all our subjects. In English, Mr Smart was looking for volunteers for the end of term play which this year was to be an abridged version of *Macbeth* and all the kids who had caused so much trouble the year before now offered their services. *He* accepted with a humble show of gratitude that we actually found quite embarrassing.

I ended up playing MacDuff and Ally was to have the starring role of Macbeth. The school plays were always a culmination of the year's work in English and a chance for the teachers to show the attending hierarchy from the school board what they had achieved.

The day arrived and everyone had worked really hard. We had costumes, make up and scenery. This was to be no Am-dram production, we knew our lines and we were pros.

The matinee was for the pupils and the evening performance was for the parents, so we were expecting the evening slot to be met with more appreciation.

The first scene involving the witches was met with jeers and catcalls. 'Hey look there's yer burd,' etc.

It was to be expected. What wasn't expected was Ally's ad-libbing. He walked onto the stage in tights, make up, cape and crown and someone in the audience shouted, 'Ya big poof.'

Ally, forgetting that the first rule of theatre is 'the show must go on', replied with great wit and professionalism, 'Right which one of you bastards said that?'

Mr Smart, in the wings, was whispering loudly to him to get on with it.

'But one of they bastards called me a poof.'

The school board members who were sitting in the front row were tut tutting and making notes.

Smart by this time was in a panic so he brought the curtain down and ran over to Ally and gave him a short sharp lecture on the principles of theatre. He reminded him who was watching plus a hint at how miserable he could make his life if he didn't get on with it in true thespian style. What he was saying was that the show must go on, because if it didn't then Ally's life wouldn't be worth living.

Ally looked at me, 'Right you watch who shouts out and we'll knock the crap out of them the morra.'

The curtain went up and my head was popped discretely round the side of the stage, but this time teachers were also dotted about the hall ready to haul any would be theatre critics out for a hiding.

The play now went without any major mishaps, apart from most of the lines being forgotten or paraphrased, and Mr Smart was congratulated by the board members. He had survived the test of his teaching skills.

The evening performance was even better and no one accused Ally of being a big poof. He went home with the success of his first big thespian adventure coursing through his veins.

About a week later I saw him running after the school magazine editor with a copy of the magazine clutched firmly in his grasp. He chased him into the toilets, so we followed them in. The editor had written a review that said Ally was so wooden he must be sponsored by Kelvin Timber, and for that we left the editor dangling from his shoelaces on the toilet door. It was our trademark punishment, which isn't easy to carry out as it requires quite a lot of cooperation from the victim. In the next issue he printed an apology saying he might just have been a wee bit hasty in his criticism.

During the last week of third year, two events occurred, the first being the Strike followed by Eddie Beattie's revenge on McConnell for belting him on his very first day at secondary. For some reason – I can't even vaguely remember why – a spate of strikes broke out in various Glasgow schools. Basically it comprised of some pupils forming a union and refusing to leave the playground and enter the classrooms.

All they did was stand en masse and chant, 'Strike . . . strike.' I don't think there were any actual demands, other than the right to gather in the playground to shout, 'Strike . . . strike.'

Winker and myself were amongst the strikers and our pals were watching events from the ground floor Biology class. The

Headmaster was out with most of the teachers, including McConnell, and they were writing down any pupils' names they could identify. Much in the same way today's police videotape protests and strikes to identify the ringleaders.

Winker and myself got lost in the crowd, watching and listening as the Headmaster's pleas and actions were becoming less patient and more animated. The Headie eventually gave up, locked the school doors and phoned the police who came in fleets of vans at high speed across the playing fields.

As they approached, those fast enough to escape got off their mark but they did manage to make a few arrests. During the melee we climbed through the window into the class and Mr Smith, rather than making a big issue out of it, just said sarcastically, 'Nice of you to join us.'

But . . . while McConnell was out in the playground in short sleeves playing Herr Kommandant, Eddie had gone into his classroom to find his jacket and belt he'd left on the back of his chair. This allowed Eddie to nail McConnell's belt to his desk, after which he sawed the legs off his chair and as a nice finishing touch he wrote, 'You're a big bastard,' on his blackboard with an aerosol.

He also, just for good measure, signed his handiwork on the blackboard with 'MM rules'. This led to every pupil with those initials being questioned and threatened by McConnell who was determined to extract a confession from someone, be they innocent or guilty. Eddie Beattie was never even suspected as the initials on the board stood for Mad Mental.

While the interrogations were going on after normal school hours, Eddie also let the tyres down on McConnell's car. McConnell went ballistic and the next day he belted (with a new belt of course) anyone who was seen striking the previous day.

He punished each pupil as though he was the culprit who had worked him over. The pupils union was abolished the day after it started. The education department had brought in their version of the army in the form of General George Patton McConnell. McConnell never did find out who was guilty but from then on he regarded every pupil as though he'd done it and treated him accordingly.

13

SO WHERE DO YOU HANG
A WET CROMBIE?

That summer we had a heatwave and we'd go down to the park to watch the girls sunbathing, trying to get as close to them as we inconspicuously could without being accused of peeping.

We were into girls in a big way and by this time we'd each had a girlfriend and knew the basics of the female form, which for a long time had been a bit of a mystery.

Now we knew that females enjoyed a winch just as much as we did. It had taken a lot of trial and error to discover this. We thought they fought us off because they hated it. Now we knew it was because they didn't want to get a reputation or get pregnant. They more than likely didn't know how to get pregnant and a pretty high percentage probably thought they'd end up with child if they rubbed a ball of baby pink wool and a knitting pattern for a baby cardigan together. Getting off with someone was done in a ritual manner, which had to be observed at all times.

We would position ourselves in easy view then hang around like a bunch of James Deans, the girls would walk past about ten times and be ignored for the first five. By the sixth we'd make inane comments, which they wouldn't acknowledge until the eighth, the acknowledgement generally came in the form of 'what are you looking at, ye want a picture?' By the tenth we were conversing quite freely and only then could the courtship commence.

When I say courtship, it was more like walking around the

streets until it got dark enough to persuade them to go round the back of the close for a winch and a fumble. I got to know more females than my mates because I was dead sneaky. Whenever anyone passed who was remotely attractive I would approach them with the ploy 'my pal fancies you'. They would ask who and I would point out Wilco sitting there in his NHS glasses and plukes visible at fifty paces. They would look at me as though I was mad and say, 'Him? He's an uggo.' Now that I'd made contact with the girls I would subliminally sell myself to them and about 10% of the time it worked.

Wilco was oblivious to the fact I was using him to break the ice and he thought I'd amazing bottle when it came to the fairer sex. On Wilco's glasses, he claimed that they weren't NHS jobs but John Lennon specials, to which Ally answered, 'Well, John Lennon must be a prick as well then.'

The nights seemed endless and the days just rolled into one another. We had no school and no worries, in fact the only weed in the garden was lack of cash. On a Saturday we'd all jump on a bus and go into the city to wander round the shops, record shops and boutiques (there's a word from the past). We could neither afford records nor clothes and all we could do was crowd into a wee booth in the record shop and try to listen to the latest releases on a single set of headphones or try on clothes way beyond our price range, which was zero anyway. We didn't really go into the shop to try clothes on anyway, we went into the shop because that shop was the Crazy House in the Gallowgate at Glasgow Cross. On Saturday the Crazy House had scantily clad go-go dancers in circular cages giving it laldy to the hits of the day and you weren't allowed simply to go in and watch them. No, the bum and boob shaking was solely a perk for customers, so the place was mobbed with, I reckon, one actual customer who intended to buy something and about a hundred other people just trying something on.

The Crazy House specialised in what I suppose could have been termed mod/skinhead gear. They sold Levi's Sta Prest,

Ben Sherman button downs, Skinner jeans and Crombie coats. Crombie's were expensive, heavy, all wool coats and as one of the go-go dancers had large nipples I heard a fellow audience member/fake shopper say, 'Jeez oh, look at them man, you could hang a wet Crombie on them.' A phrase that was both very descriptive and incredibly accurate. I'd love to say that the go-go dancers were exotic, but they weren't. They were Glaswegian go-go dancers and if there's words that shouldn't appear in the same sentence it's 'Glaswegian' and 'go-go' and 'dancers'. They were a bit dumpy is what I'm saying. Think Lulu back in the sixties when she had the baw face and the fat legs and that's about the strength of it.

Our weekly sojourns were a welcome diversion. We didn't mind weekdays because we'd have been at school anyway but shouldn't we do something even more special on a Saturday than simple window shopping? Going into Glasgow, or the town as it was put, was and still is a Glaswegian ritual. Most of the time it's just to wander about aimlessly, a ritual that's lasted for years and will continue I'm sure for many years more.

The money problem was overcome when we went out and found ourselves jobs as paperboys and milk boys. With a bit of cash we decided we'd have enough to go to a disco in the city centre once a month.

Not that we knew much about discos but we wanted to find out.

You see we believed what we'd seen on the telly and thought that every nightclub was like the ones Simon Templar – the Saint – went to. There would be lots of girls in yellow plastic miniskirts dancing on tables and everyone would be kissing each other.

So, with cash in pocket, four shiny-faced kids set off for the bright lights on the number 41 bus. We got off the bus at the old Buchanan Street bus station and made for the first pub that caught our eye – The Tri-anon in Sauchiehall Street. The first obstacle was the bouncers but they were both involved in chatting up a couple of girls so they just glanced in our direction and nodded us in.

This pub was unlike the only other pub I'd visited. It was lively, loud and full of people who looked roughly our own age. Ally went away and got three lagers and a coke. The coke was for me as I remembered my first alcohol experiment and didn't want a repeat performance. Ally said we should position ourselves next to the ladies toilets as sooner or later every girl in the place would have to go wee wee, that way we could check out the talent without wandering about bumping into people and looking like desperados.

No one even looked at us and, disappointed, we left as last orders were called at a quarter to ten. The Scottish Parliament go on and on about binge drinking and the causes of it. What caused it then was everyone tanning whatever they could shove down their neck to get blootered before the pubs shut at ten o'clock.

The only disco we knew of at the time was Clouds, which was situated six floors above the Apollo. We got to the door and casually sauntered in. We'd got about three feet when a large Neanderthal stepped into our path.

'Whit age are ye?'

'Eighteen.'

'Any ID?'

'Any idea of what?'

'Look yeez arenae eighteen, piss off.'

Usually when you weren't in possession of ID they'd try to catch you out by asking you your date of birth, which you'd taken three years off to make you eighteen and memorised. We must have looked so young that even knowing the exact date of our fake date of birth wouldn't have made any difference. I don't know why the entrance age was eighteen because Clouds wasn't even licensed to sell drink.

Crestfallen, we went outside. Ally was all for going back in to challenge the bouncers to a square go. Winker just said, 'Aye sure.' At least he wasn't shouting what I've heard many people shout since, which is, 'I pay your wages.'

'Cannae get in eh?' A half drunk guy who must have been in his early twenties approached us asking what happened.

Ally informed him, 'The big fat bunter stopped us.'

The guy went on to give us his advice.

'Aye well yeez shouldnae go in mob handed cos the bouncers don't like too many single guys in ye know. Look, whit yeez dae is go roon the corner, swop yer jaikets and get a haud of a couple of bints and ask to go in with them, that confuses the bastards nae end.'

'What's a bint?'

'You know burds, touche, nanny, fanny, know.'

We'd nothing to lose so took his advice and went round the corner and swopped jackets. Once done we pleaded with any passing girls to get us in and Ally and Wilco had success first and strolled in by the bouncers with girls on their arms.

'Christ sake it works, mon, here's two coming noo.'

Two girls were heading our way from about forty yards down the street. They looked quite small from so far away but with each step towards us they got taller. Once alongside us they were both about a foot taller than Winker and myself. They both looked like a couple of whores in distress but what did we know.

'Hey missus, gonnie get us into Clouds?'

'Who you calling missus?'

'Sorry can you get us in?'

'Whit age are youse?'

'Eighteen.'

'Yer arse, I've done farts that have been aboot longer than you.'

Her pal, silent until now, took pity on us.

'Aw come on Isa, gie the wee boys a chance.'

Isa looked at us.

'Aye awright then, but if yeez get papped don't blame us.'

SO WHERE DO YOU HANG A WET CROMBIE?

So they took our arms and we headed back round the corner, I caught sight of our foursome in a shop window and the scene looked ridiculous. The arrangement looked hopeless and on entering, the bouncer put his arm out and stopped us.

'Aye right.'

We thought our chances were zero but Isa came to our rescue.

'C'mon Erchie ye were young yersel wance, gie the boys a chance.'

But Erchie still said no.

'Come tae grips man, the place is full of under-agers anyway, so what difference is another two gonnie fuckin' make.'

I'll say one thing for Isa, she had a certain je ne sais quoi about her.

The bouncer dithered a bit, then looked straight at us.

'Aye all right. Just this wance but any bother and I'll toe yer arses all the way oot.'

We thanked him profusely, paid the entrance fee and got in the lift to take us the five floors up to the club. On the journey Isa told us, 'Right we got yeez in but don't start pestering us up here awright, we don't want any of oor pals tae think we hing about wae afterbirth, awright.'

Once in the club we hunted down Ally and Wilco and found them standing self-consciously at the bottom of the stairs leading to the dance floor.

'Yeez got in then,' said Ally very half-heartedly as his confidence and sparkle had disappeared.

'What's up wae you?'

'We've been standing here watching everybody go down to the dance floor.'

'So?'

'Well the place is hoaching wae posing bastards wae all the best gear and haircuts. I mean look at us. I've got a suit on that doesnae fit me, Joe 90 here is horsed before he starts and youse two look as though ye've shoplifted your clothes out of Oxfam. We'll never get burds in here, we've nae chance.'

133

Wilco then said something he must have read on the back of a matchbox: 'Faint heart never won fair lady.'

Ally looked at him as though he was going to belt him: 'Shuttit fannybaws.'

Winker was a bit more constructive.

'Well Ally, ye can stand here if you want but I didnae pay one and a half quid to hang around the bottom of the stairs, Christ I can dae that at the bottom of the close for nothing.' He beckoned to me, 'Come on.'

I looked at Ally and Wilco, shrugged my shoulders and followed Winker into the club. The music was deafening and one minute the floor was totally illuminated and the next it was pitch black, disco lights apparently.

The dancers were grouped in the middle of the dance floor and we stood at the side watching. Those not dancing were wandering aimlessly in a circle round the dance floor.

'How come everyone's walking round and round?' I asked Winker.

We soon found out when a bouncer appeared at our side.

'If you're no dancing boys ye'll need to keep moving.' He then ushered us to join the circle. I still don't know why everyone had to walk round and round and can only assume that the bouncers didn't like loitering.

After about ten laps we decided it was time for a dance. We spied two girls dancing alone. Winker headed towards them, stopped for a second and shouted in my ear above the din. 'Right we'll start with a couple of howlers and work our way up.'

I followed him and tapped the girl on the shoulder. She turned, didn't even acknowledge my presence and started dancing facing me.

Winker's choice did the same.

We'd have been as well not being there as they both gave the best impressions of someone dancing alone when they have a partner that I have ever seen.

SO WHERE DO YOU HANG A WET CROMBIE?

The record seemed to go on forever and neither Winker nor myself could think of a lead line to break the ice, the record finished after what seemed like an eternity and the two of us left the dance floor at high speed.

'No exactly friendly up here are they,' said Winker.

I could offer no explanation so I just nodded and said nothing.

He went on, 'At least at the school dances we're popular. Maybe Ally's right, we are out of our depth up here.'

Right on cue Ally appeared with Wilco in tow. He was excited.

'Wait till you see this, it's fucking brilliant, mon.'

He led us up the stairs and up to the balcony. Clouds had a balcony right round the dance floor, which was full of intimate alcoves.

He led us round and each alcove housed a couple giving it mad winching.

'So what,' said Winker.

'Naw, roon here a bit, just look but for fucks sake don't stop, just keep going.'

We reached the alcove that Ally was talking about and found a couple actually engaged in the sex act. We hurried by at a snail's pace and out of earshot of the couple Ally asked the obvious question.

'Did you fucking see that? Fucking hell.'

'Aye, mon let's go back round again.'

We made four more passes and on the fifth they'd finished and were sitting smoking cigarettes.

The show was over.

'Christ sakes,' said Winker. 'Let's go downstairs and find some mad shaggers.'

As luck would have it the Alcove Don Juan must have acquired the only rampant nymphomaniac in the place, but we did leave the disco a lot older and a lot wiser than we were two hours previously.

We walked down to George Square to catch the one o'clock

late bus home. It was our first après midnight visit to the Square and we were astonished at some of the sights. Drunks lay everywhere, people were fighting and yelling gang slogans and swearing at each other and car loads of posers were driving around and asking girls if they'd like a lift home. There were a lot of policemen around but they were just standing in groups talking to each other and ignoring everything happening around them.

The atmosphere reeked of violence and intimidation. One drunk started shouting abuse at the cops and that's the last thing you want to do to members of Strathclyde Police Force. He was yelling, 'Calton Young Team, come intae me,' at the police. The Calton Young Team were a big gang, but no matter how many members the Calton Young Team had, the biggest gang in Glasgow was and still is Strathclyde Police Force. Their motto is Semper Vigilis, which is latin for 'We're More Mental Than You'll Ever Be'. Eventually though the cops got fed up with listening to the drunk Caltonite and he was grabbed and thrown head first into the back of a Black Maria and taken off to the police station, where no doubt the next morning he'd have awoken covered in black and blue bruises caused by him accidentally falling down the stairs in the police station a few times.

We joined the bus queue and tried hard not to catch anyone's eye as we wanted to remain as anonymous as possible. When the bus did arrive there was chaos. The buses then were still open backed and everyone rushed to get on it. People were pushing and shoving, and swearing and when it did eventually leave it was carrying twice the recommended passengers. Even so, latecomers were running after it still trying to board even though there was absolutely no room to even get a foot up on the back end platform. I'd seen footage of the last days of the Vietnam War with people on the roof of the American Embassy trying to get on helicopters. That's what the late night number 10 bus looked like – the Glasgow version of the last chopper out of Saigon.

SO WHERE DO YOU HANG A WET CROMBIE?

The thud of the music was still throbbing in my head. All the way home I could feel it and when my head hit the pillow it kept me awake long enough to reflect on the night's events.

I had visited my first grown up disco, I had seen my first sex act and I had survived my first late night in George Square. I fell asleep with mixed feelings.

We made many more forays to the bright lights after that and every one was a battle of contrition with the bouncers. Sometimes they let us in and other times they didn't and there was no point in trying the other clubs because we were far too young for the Electric Garden and even at the age of fifteen/sixteen we were far too old for Terminal One. We did one time go to the White Elephant in Sauchiehall Street but got into a fight and were thrown out. The bouncers told us not to even attempt to get back in because we were barred and as they informed us 'the Elephant never forgets'. Not getting into Clouds didn't always mean a ruined night because downstairs was the Apollo and if you failed the club entrance exam you could always take in a gig. After one Clouds knockback we went to see the Electric Light Orchestra and after another knockback we got into the sell out Fleetwood Mac concert. It was sold out, but for £1 the bouncer would hand you a raffle ticket as a ticket and sneak you in through a fire exit. You didn't get a seat and you had to look as though you were either coming from or going to the toilets to stop the bouncer's bosses from finding out that the hall was way, way, way beyond its legal capacity.

14

WELL NOBODY'S PREFECT ARE THEY?

We returned to school that August as the crème de la crème – our words, not Miss Jean Brodie's. There were only twenty-three of us left out of the 120 or so who had commenced first year, which, of course, is a very small percentage and this had advantages and disadvantages.

The pros being that the teaching was much more intense, and the cons being that in times of trouble it would be extremely difficult to get lost amongst the throng.

During morning assembly the Headmaster called out a list of names of those who were to report to his office after registration and Winker's and mine were tagged on last. We hadn't had any time to get up to any mischief so we were a bit confused about why he wanted to see us.

We found out – he wanted to make us prefects and we of course declined because prefects are usually crawley bummie licks and we didn't want to be tarred with the same brush. He insisted, in fact he insisted strongly, saying it would build our character and with no option we left his presence sporting our badges of office.

We entered our first class of the term, Miss Goudie's history double period. She was in the middle of her 'how dare you come into my class late' speech when we flashed our badges, 'School polis mam.' She then accused us of stealing them and it took quite a bit of convincing that the badges were genuine authorised issue. She was as incredulous as we were of the dubious honour accorded us.

WELL NOBODY'S PREFECT ARE THEY?

During the break Winker outlined the plan he had been working on in History to get us the sack as prefects and out of the extra work involved and that lunchtime we put the plan into action. One of the duties was to station ourselves at the bottom of the two sets of stairs leading up to the classrooms and direct first years to their lessons. At one stair I succeeded in sending a whole class of first years to Blairtummock primary school half a mile away by telling them we were using it as a school annexe. Winker for his part sent thirty pupils to the Headmaster for misbehaving and he also gave the first-year Geography class the afternoon off because the teacher was off sick.

The result was chaos.

The Headmistress from the primary school phoned to say she had found an entire class wandering her corridors, the pupils sent to the Headie were wandering about lost because they had no idea where the Headie's office was, and the Geography class had disappeared completely into a parallel dimension.

Winker and I were sitting in the common room on a free period when we were summoned.

We knocked on his door, he debadged us, called us a couple of morons and said he was giving us a week's detention.

'What's detention, Sir?' asked Winker.

The belt was to be phased out as much as possible this term and replacing it would be detention classes. This meant a class laid aside for an extra hour's schooling each night as a punishment. We had been sentenced to five.

As we left his office Winker didn't seem too bothered.

'It's only an hour, it'll be a laugh.'

I looked at him, 'But a whole week?'

'We'll have been pardoned by Wednesday. They'll have some poor diddy student in charge and he'll not be able to handle it.'

He couldn't have been more wrong because on entering the detention class we found McConnell positioned behind the desk.

'Typical, I wondered how long it would take you two to end up in here.'

He warned us in no uncertain terms what would happen and basically told us that he'd bury us in a shallow grave if we gave him any grief.

Apparently he was not one of the corporal punishment reformers.

Winker and I stared at the clock whilst he did the *Glasgow Herald* crossword. Every so often he would look up to see if we were misbehaving before returning to his paper.

That went on for the whole week, an hour's silence each night. Winker and I were the only pupils and this was almost the pattern for the entire term.

Being fourth years we now had a common room, which was a great place to hide if you were dodging lessons. It had a telly, which for some reason only ever picked up educational programmes, a table tennis table and a dartboard.

Darts became a great favourite until someone stuck a dart in the school captain's bum and the armoury was removed.

Winker would pull the valves out of the telly and throw them four floors to the ground to hear them going off with a bang. No matter how many valves he removed somehow the telly still worked. Obviously they don't make them like that anymore.

We had fewer classes now as we had all picked the subjects we wanted to specialise in and concentrated on those subjects. But to sit the O-grades, the prelims had to be passed first.

That year the school board had introduced a new grading system, for instance:

A pass = 85% and over

B pass = 75% and over

C pass = 50% and over

D pass = 40% and over

E pass = 30% and over

There was a catch however. Although you'd have to be a complete dunce to fail, to get any sort of pass you could only sit the O-grade if you achieved 50% or over in the prelims. Much is made of the dumbing down of exams nowadays, and in my opinion they must be dumbed down. In recent exams it was reported that 97% of pupils had passed their Maths O-levels. 97%? Aye, so they completely and utterly did.

A lack of teachers in the seventies meant you couldn't sit O-levels in every subject. At least I'm assuming that was the reason. For instance you couldn't sit Geography and History, it was one or the other. In science you could either sit Chemistry or Biology, not both. And it was just too bad if you required both Chemistry and Biology O-levels and then Highers for the university course you wanted to move on to.

We settled down to our studies and I still couldn't understand bloody algebra, maybe it's simple when you get the gist of it, you know the wee tricks, but it was and still is totally beyond me.

In all our classes we had a few fifth years repeating the subjects they had failed the O-grade in. Of course, there was no shame in this, except in Arithmetic.

Failing in Arithmetic was the same as contracting leprosy and we had two resident lepers. Our teacher in this subject was a small but muscular Malaysian man who we called Precious McKenzie because he looked like Precious McKenzie the Commonwealth champion weightlifter.

Arithmetic is basic common sense, two plus two equals four, but our two lepers couldn't quite comprehend this difficult equation. Every time they were asked a question in class the room would fall silent to hear their comedy gem of an answer.

Leper One was gRant and although the hippy era had drawn to a close he hadn't noticed. It was rumoured that LSD was responsible for his dull wit and low intelligence. His one redeeming aspect was that he was a brilliant artist and the reason he was still at school was to gain enough passes to get into art school. No doubt for a career in illustrating *Noggin the Nog*.

From what I've seen since leaving school and what now passes for art, gRant should have been able to get in with a metalwork O-level, that and an ability to talk a complete load of bollocks.

Leper Two was Thuggie Millar whose name was actually Shuggie but he had a world class lisp, he could have lisped for Scotland. Thuggie's ambition was to go to Sandhurst for Officer training. He had overdosed on *Commando* comics.

Precious, I think, felt sorry for Thuggie and indeed there was a lot to feel sorry for as he had the lot. Short hair, thick neck, thick lips, unlevel ears and his eyes were looking permanently in different directions. One was almost looking at you while the other was away to the shops for sweeties.

Precious would spend a lot of time on Thuggie just trying to make him understand. 'If I have one apple in this hand and I take it away, how many apples would I have?' Nine out of ten times he got it wrong.

There was no higher Arithmetic as it only went as far as O-grade and was classed as an easy subject. As yet, no one in the school had failed it twice but these two were sure candidates.

In fourth year we now had to visit the Careers Officer in order for him to advise us and give us help to achieve our gainful employment dreams. Of course we were still at the age of wanting to be pop stars and footballers, with the girls coming a close second in the fantasy stakes as air hostesses. The Careers Officer was an intolerant man who was always throwing pupils out of his office and telling them to return when they'd grown up: 'Bloody pop star, indeed.'

Winker, on his visit, told him that he'd like to be a careers officer. He'd meant it as a joke but the C.O. took him seriously and all through fourth year bombarded him with leaflets and application forms.

I told the C.O. that I would like to be a dentist. It was the first thing that sprang to mind as I had just visited one that morning and he had a gorgeous receptionist. He took one look at my reports and told me to set my aim a bit lower, well a lot lower actually, and waved me out of his office after handing me a wad of pamphlets on employment in Cowglen Savings Bank.

The pamphlets featured pictures of happy faces seated at desks with big broad smiles and articles on the Cowglen Tennis Club, the Cowglen Badminton Club, the Cowglen Highland Dancing Club and the prospects within the Civil Service for the dedicated civil servant.

'YES – YOU can have a glowing career in banking.'

The pamphlets ended up in the bin. Especially since they mentioned badminton because badminton is pathetic, it's just tennis for people with weak arms.

In October we had the 'egg incident', which led to me and Winker being expelled. We were in Nutty's science class for the last double period of the week and Nutty had to leave the room for five minutes. While he was away, Winker strolled down to Nutty's desk, took an egg out of his pocket, cracked it open with a ruler and poured the contents on Nutty's textbook. Winker shut the book and returned to his seat.

Everyone in the class looked at him as though he was mad.

'What did you do that for?'

'Dunno.'

Nutty returned to the class and told us to open our books at page fifty-two. Nutty opened his book and the egg dribbled out and onto his desk.

He went completely, completely mental.

He shouted, 'Who's responsible for this?' in a voice so many octaves higher than his normal voice that only dogs could hear him.

There was total silence, because we weren't dogs after all, were we?

'I said which one of you bloody wee bastards did this?'

Ally went, 'Woooooooooo, you swore Sir.'

'Right Dixon, out now.'

He tried to give Ally two of the belt but he kept parting his hands at the last second and the belt flew harmlessly in between them. This made him worse. He screamed again: 'Who did this?'

Winker wouldn't own up and no one pointed the finger.

Nutty then went round checking everyone's bags for evidence of eggs.

I opened mine and about half a ton of red ash fell out.

'Sorry sir, red ash sir, my football boots are in the bag.'

He went round the whole class and found nothing so he sent someone to get the Housemaster Mr Nesbitt.

Nesbitt came in looking weary as an awful lot of the trouble in the school came from Nutty's Chemistry class. Nutty showed him the book and said, 'I'll get to the bottom of this if these swine have to stay here all weekend.'

Mr Nesbitt addressed the class resignedly, 'If the culprit owns up now it will save everyone a lot of time and trouble.'

No one's eyes moved and we all sat and stared straight ahead. We all thought that the whole class being punished was worth it just to see Nutty's rampant indignation.

Mr Nesbitt had a plan and as it happened it was a very, very good plan. He took all the pupils along to the common room and interviewed us one by one in his office next door.

My turn came.

'Did you see anything?'

'No sir.'

'Is that all you have to say?'

'Yes sir.'

He knew that the most dominant members of the class wouldn't talk but there were others who would. He could have got the information at any point but he interviewed every class member anyway to allay suspicion. After it was all over Winker and myself were told to stay behind.

The other pupils left for home and none of them could look us in the eye except Ally who said, 'Aw well, there you go eh.'

We stood looking out of the window.

'I wonder who grassed ye Wink?'

'Havenae got a scooby.'

I had no idea why I was there, after all I hadn't actually done anything.

Nutty came in with Nesbitt. Nutty was all for giving us a thrashing but Nesbitt just said matter of factly that we were both expelled.

'Both expelled!' said Winker. 'He didn't do it, I did.'

Nutty growled that I was his accomplice.

'Aye, right enough, sir, it was him who laid the egg.'

The humour and injustice of Winker's statement was lost on Nutty.

Nesbitt beckoned us into his office and handed us notes to give to our parents to explain why we were being booted out.

'Look, sir, it was a joke.' I thought for one horrible minute he was going to say yolk. It would have been on his mind but on this occasion he declined to be humorous.

'We didn't mean any harm.'

'That's as maybe Watson but it's too late for apologies.'

'So what happens now sir?'

He explained that we were to pay for the book, make hand-written sorries to Nutty and return with our parents who would then be informed of our behaviour.

I was innocent so I started to protest.

'But sir, I didn't do anything.'

'Yes, but there are varying degrees of guilt, Watson is your pal and you didn't try to stop him did you?'

There was no answer to such logic. As we left his office Winker apologised.

'Helluva sorry about this wee man.'

The weekend was spent trying to explain my innocence to my parents who received my denials with the usual disbelief. My father said that there was no smoke without fire – now he was also accusing me of arson.

My parents were never the type to run up to the school to complain that somebody had belted their wee boy. I suppose they were parents of that era. Nowadays teachers always seem to be having charges of assault laid against them by parents of wee angels. No, mine were of the attitude that if I was belted it was for a good reason. They were right. Seems today's kids can do no wrong.

Monday morning came and we appeared in front of the Headie with our mums and dads and both my dad and Winker's were angry that they were missing work. You'd have thought we were at the Old Bailey and the judge was wearing a black cap the way our parents sucked up to the Headmaster.

The Headmaster for his part said that we obviously came from good homes and we were an embarrassment to our families. I just sat there thinking that, probably for the first time, I hadn't actually done anything. So where was Emile Zola to write a J'accuse open letter to the school board when I needed him?

The book had to be paid for, which it was, and after we had written and delivered our apologies to Nutty the matter would be closed. So, school honour satisfied, the parents left and Winker and I trotted off to Nutty's class with our hastily scribbled notes.

We knocked on his classroom door and entered.

He had a class full of first years who were sitting in the usual frightened silence. Nutty looked at us with extreme distaste.

We handed over our notes, which he read and threw straight into the bin.

'If I had my way I would have had both of you taken outside and shot.'

Winker piped up, 'Not legal any more sir.'

'What?' growled Nutty.

'Murder sir, not legal anymore.'

'Get out!' he shouted.

As we were leaving I whispered under my breath, 'Wanker.'

Nutty shot out of his desk and came after me and grabbed me by the hair.

WELL NOBODY'S PREFECT ARE THEY?

'What did you just say?'

'Winker sir, that's Watson's nickname.'

He opened the door and shoved us both out into the corridor.

'You pair of thugs, I promise you that if I ever catch you at anything ever again I'll skin you alive and Nesbitt won't stop me.'

He went back into his room and slammed the door.

As we walked back along the corridor Winker spoke, 'That man's gonnie give himself a stroke so he is.'

We sat our prelims in December and eagerly awaited the results as it was the first time that we had learned they would have any direct bearing on our futures. The exams were conducted in a room with the desks placed a few feet apart, out of whisper range, and an adjudicator roamed up and down the aisles to watch for cheating. We were given an hour and a half to complete each exam and I was confident that I would pass everything except Maths.

During Maths I sat and scratched my head while Spig, a pupil who carried his books in a briefcase, sat in the adjacent desk scribbling away like a demon, I thought to myself, 'What a bastard.'

I had written my name on the paper and little else. The rest was as usual totally beyond me . . . y plus x equals what. Nope, haven't got a scooby. After about half an hour I thought that I'd better write something on the exam paper so without any rhyme or reason I started writing answers which probably bore no relation to the question. I lived in hope.

On Arithmetic I sailed through and was supremely confident that I'd passed. I finished the paper with half an hour to go and spent the remainder of the time sniggering at the facial expressions of the two arithmetic lepers who looked as lost as ever. Me, I was good at this, so good I hadn't even put my workings down on the paper. I was putting the mental into mental arithmetic.

The results were due in January after the Christmas break so we'd have a good Christmas and worry about the outcome in the New Year.

The school dances were looming and due to lack of people in fourth, fifth and sixth year we would have to amalgamate for the purpose of filling the hall. We were to play the gig accompanied by a mobile disco worked by Tiger Tim Stevens. Tim had risen to fame after a stint as a contestant on the telly game show *The Sky's the Limit*.

Tim lived across the back from me and we'd played football many times prior to his telly debut but he had never cracked a light about it to any of us. When the news broke that he'd been on the telly he became the butt of a million inane jokes. Of course he didn't help his street cred by getting posters printed with the words 'star of *The Sky's the Limit*' on them. I periodically still hear from Tim and in the early nineties we even did a radio panto together in which I played the roles of Taggart and Rambo. I won't bore you with details but the show was taped and Tim lent me the mastercopy, which I promptly lost. So, every so often I get a call from Tim asking me if I've found the tape, and each time I tell him that it's lost, lost forever. In fact, as lost things go, this is the most lost anything has ever been. This doesn't stop Tim periodically phoning looking for it and the last tape inquiry was made between the hours of 1pm and 3pm on Sunday, 4 July 2009. I know the exact date because I was having my son Joshua christened by the Reverend Kenneth Main at the Old Martyrs Church in Paisley and I'd left my mate Lorraine in my house to deal with the caterers. On my return she informed me that Tiger Tim had called and left the message that he was going to kick my c*** in. That's not only a terrible word that I never use or write in its full entirety, but it's also in my case anatomically completely incorrect. But that's Tim for you, never a man to let biological impossibilities get in the way of a good threat.

The band had gone through a few changes since we played our previous school dance glory gig. Ronnie had left after contracting some brain virus or another and had to spend six months in the

Southern General. Kenny and I went to see him and the steroid treatment he was receiving had made his eyes look as though they were popping out of his head. Even so he was still the least ill person on his ward as there was some sorry sights, and it was quite frightening seeing all the people with shaved heads and enormous scars. I tried not to stare but no matter how hard I tried my eyes were strangely drawn.

Ally told us he was leaving the band because his new girlfriend had told him to because she didn't like us. We referred to her forever after that as Yoko. Kenny's father had forbidden him with the warning that 'damn banjos, tarts and education don't mix'. As Kenny's father was really scary I'd have heeded his warning too. Kenny's dad was so scary that when I was up at Kenny's with a girl I'd been dating a couple of weeks and he came into the bedroom and asked, 'And who's this young lady?' him just even talking to me put me into a state of panic and I could not remember her name. My mind went completely blank and I prefer to blame the fear Kenny's father instilled rather than me simply not bothering to learn her name off by heart. She wasn't really that good looking and was really just one of those stop-gap girls you go about with until something better comes along. And she would have remained my interim love interest if she hadn't chucked me for not knowing what she was called. Talk about touchy.

There's a great Warren Zevon song called 'Looking for the Next Best Thing'. This could have been whatever-her-name-was's theme song.

My musical interlude did pay off eventually when I co-wrote two songs with Michael Mara for a Wildcat theatre show. I'd always been a fan of Michael Mara and I was chuffed to bits with the opportunity to work with him. I remember the two songs well, but I'm willing to bet he doesn't.

Romance, if you could indeed get it, was a funny thing, full of holding hands, making plans for the future and being in love, or at least thinking you were. The first really romantic couple in our year was Linda Brady and Gordon 'Gags' Thomson, who became known as the Puke Twins. God, they made everyone sick eating each other's faces in the common room, the goo-goo eyes they made at each other in the classrooms and the writing of each other's names on their school bags in big enormous letters covered by a love heart.

Ally viewed the spectacle with more distaste than the rest of us. 'He's a big poof,' said Ally.

Winker didn't agree with this, 'Well how come he's got a burd then?'

Ally explained, 'That's just a front in't it. I mean look at his hair, he tongs it and in my book that makes him a poof.'

Winker was still confused, 'I don't get it.'

'Look,' Ally went on, 'the first thing poofs dae is to get themselves a burd to allay suspicion, everyone knows that.'

We were still a bit lost.

'Well whit about the guys who've got burds and arenae poofs then?'

'Look don't confuse the issue, I'm telling ye the guy's a poof, have ye seen him in the shower after P.E., he's always first in and last oot. He's a knob watcher.'

Winker wouldn't believe it. 'You're only jealous cos he's going out with Linda Brady and you're not.'

'Aye right, I widnae have her in a Lucky Bag.'

About a week later it was rumoured that Linda was pregnant, even though she wasn't. She missed her period and had told her pal Jenny Fraser in confidence and Jenny had told me in confidence. I might have mentioned it to other people and they couldn't keep a secret. In other words, I can keep a secret, the people I tell can't. Her missed period refuelled the discussion.

'So what,' said Ally. 'I could get a burd up the duff if I wanted tae, he's still a big poof.'

Gags was a big guy and when he heard that Ally was slinging aspersions in his direction he beat him up. All Ally would say after his humiliating doing was that he couldn't fight him properly cos he was too busy protecting his arse in case Gags tried to shag him. He wasn't believed.

Bullying was part of the normal school curriculum, usually a double period on a Friday afternoon. The bigger boys bullying the smaller boys, the smaller boys bullying the tiny boys and the tiny boys bullying insects and small woodland creatures.

It was all done on a descending scale and as I fell into the category of the smaller boys I was bullied by a couple of fat blokes called Tanya and Panda. These two would waddle about the school looking like Oliver Hardy and Oliver Hardy and neither had any bone in their body that any rational person could reason with.

They would pick on people incessantly with varying degrees of malice but one day they came up with this idea of turning bullying into a profit.

This wasn't their first profitable operation though. Their previous at primary was to get a hold of your head and rub their knuckles into your scalp until you coughed up any money in your possession. Which was never much so it was actually only very marginally profitable. But if you factor in all the time and effort they went to they were probably running at a slight loss.

The knuckle rubbing was painful and the pre-runner for the hairdresser's shiatsu massage they torture you with nowadays prior to a haircut.

This time their latest bullying venture, however, was much more cunning. So cunning that I'm sure the Dragons in *Dragon's Den* would have invested in it. Tanya's sister worked in the Penguin biscuit factory and one day Tanya and Panda brought into the school a large bag of broken Penguins, which they offered around.

We had our suspicions and thought that they might be laced with rat poison or whatever, but one pupil who was trying to curry favour with them ate one to please them. He never suffered any ill effects so we delved in.

Our suspicions were indeed justified, for about a week later they came into the school demanding money for the biscuits we'd eaten. Anyone not paying up found themselves on the receiving end of a doing.

Most paid up including Wilco, but Winker, Ally and myself refused despite the threats. We figured if we stayed together it would be three against two, which weren't great odds but they were better than giving them money we didn't actually have. I did have money but I was saving up for an Argent LP.

This plan worked fine until I had a Physics class with them and Winker and Ally were elsewhere. They approached me in the class before the teacher arrived in the room and demanded their money. Because the classroom was full of girls my mouth and my brain didn't confer and I said to them, 'Fuck off ya pair of fat bastards.'

Tanya hit me across the face with a metre stick and I went down beside a fire bucket. Panda reached into the bucket and scooped up a handful of sand and threw it in my face, which was by then covered in blood. They'd caught me across the bridge of my nose with the stick and to this day I still have the scar to remind me, in times of mortal danger, to keep my mouth well and truly shut. By the time the teacher came in I was dabbing the blood and sand off my face with a hankie. Not being a grass I told the teacher I had fallen into the bucket. I was well pissed off but would have to wait for back up to seek revenge.

I didn't wait long. The next day Winker, Ally and myself hid in a recess on the second floor corridor and waited till Tanya and Panda had passed heading towards the stairs. We sneaked after them and when they both had one foot in the air to descend to the first step we rushed forward and pushed them both head-long down the stairs.

As they tumbled down with pencils, books and biscuits flying everywhere, we made our escape unseen. Both of them escaped with just bruises but justice, we felt, had been served. They couldn't prove who'd done it but had their suspicions and very much left us alone after that.

15

FORTY-FIVE AND A QUARTER DEGREES

During the winter break I attended my first non-smarty party, that is to say that there was drink there, real drink and not some alcoholic poison that Ally provided. I didn't imbibe as I still remembered too well what had happened on the previous occasion. Everyone else, however, ended up blitzed or at the very least a bit more tipsy. We played Postman's Knock and Spin the Bottle, games designed to help the shy amongst us forget our inane patter and cut to the winching. I ended up in an embrace with Slack Alice – this name was not based on observations of her sexual exploits but because she had a loose brace on her front teeth. Every time we kissed my filling touched her metal brace and I almost shot through the roof in pain. As usual there were those who had drunk too much and the smell of vomit became so overpowering that I had to go out on the veranda every so often to get some fresh air. On the subject of air, I adopted an air of pompous superiority, 'Well you shouldn't really have drunk so much, you were bound to be sick weren't you?'

And, 'You know you shouldn't really have to drink to enjoy yourself.'

Ally after one bout with his head down the pan looked up at me sitting next to him on the bath and said, 'You'd better fuck up.' His head then went back into the pan and he barfed up what looked like most of his lower intestine. It was kind of a weird party musically. The host of the party's entire record collection comprised of Barbra Streisand, Bette Midler and

Musicals LP's and it was only many years later, when I discovered that certain sections of society like Barbra Streisand, Bette Midler and show tunes, that the penny dropped and it explained why the host excused himself from spin the bottle.

In January we returned for the new term and to our prelim results. I passed every subject except Maths, Arithmetic and Physics. Failing in Maths was a foregone conclusion as I been awarded 7%, and that was about 7% more than I'd expected to get, but failing in Arithmetic certainly wasn't.

Precious told me the bad news that I had scored 30% as he handed me the paper. I looked at it and all the answers were correct so I was puzzled and demanded to know why I hadn't been given full marks.

'Because you never showed how you worked the answers out.'

I went into indignant mode.

'What do you mean I didn't work the answers out, I did, I worked them out in my fuckin' head.'

He gave me two weeks detention for swearing but I still wouldn't let it go. He was yelling at me to sit down and I was yelling that I wouldn't until he reconsidered the mark.

'This isn't fair sir, the answers are right, what the fuck does it matter how I got them?'

He gave me another week.

In all I got two months detention before he backed down and gave me a pass. To him it had got past the stage of being worth the bother. I had gained a pass but lost my freedom.

Back in the Maths class Tranny said he was disappointed in me, adding that algebra was like riding a bike, once you had figured out the basics, the rest was easy.

I looked up from glancing indifferently over my paper.

'They say the same about shagging sir.'

Tranny being deaf didn't hear me but the class did and went into laughter with Tranny joining in, oblivious to what he was laughing at.

FORTY-FIVE AND A QUARTER DEGREES

I failed my Physics prelim miserably too and for me the subject was another complete waste of time, and not just my time but the teacher's time too. The Physics teacher was a highly-strung man we called Shazzan because he had a goatee beard and looked like one of the characters on the Arabian Nights segment on *The Banana Splits* show. He had the wrong temperament for teaching and after trying to teach kids who wouldn't listen, he was at the end of his tether, and I just happened to be in his class for a double period when the end of his tether was reached and his tether audibly snapped.

He had asked the class a question and everyone was shouting out answers.

'A million sir.'

'A cabbage.'

'Forty-five and a quarter degrees sir.'

'Tuesday.'

He shouted above the melee, 'Right who said forty-five and a quarter degrees?'

Thinking that it was the right answer and although I hadn't said it I was going to take the credit for it, I stuck my hand up.

'Me sir.'

He flipped and dragged me out of my seat, out into the corridor and began to belt me with a vengeance.

I protested my innocence, I was the one who shouted out cabbage and surely that was a stupider answer than the one I was being punished for. He continued to belt me. Mr Smart, an English teacher in the adjacent classroom, heard the smacks and assumed he must be belting the whole class and came out to give him a hand.

When Mr Smart saw that only one pupil was on the receiving end, he ran along and grabbed the belt from the by now slabbering at the mouth Shazzan.

'For God's sake man, what has he done?'

Smart must have thought that I'd assassinated the whole class to merit this.

Shazzan was shouting, 'He said forty-five and a quarter degrees!'

He was still trying to get at me and Smart had to hold him back. Shazzan had lost it completely. I thought so, as did Mr Smart. I was ordered back into the classroom and told to wait there while Smart took Shazzan off to see the Headie. I opened the classroom door and all those who had been behind it scurried back to their seats. A cheer went up.

Shuggie said I had been given thirteen strokes but Winker said it had been fourteen. Winker was the smartest so I believed him. If Winker was right, I'd set a new school record. On the downside though, ugly wheals were starting to appear from my wrists right up to my elbows because everything happened so quickly that I didn't even have the time to roll my sleeves down to my wrists – which was what you did when getting the belt to limit the target area. I was checking my wheals when a relief teacher entered the class and told me to report to the Head-master.

I wandered off fully expecting another thumping.

I knocked on the door and a smiling headmaster opened it and bade me to sit down. He then told me that he regretted the incident and asked me if I would be taking the matter further. I wondered what he meant. Obviously he assumed that I would tell my parents and they in turn would kick up a stink in the education department.

Actually he was very straight with me. He said that my punishment far exceeded what the department deemed reasonable, then he got to the point. Would I be charging Shazzan with assault?

We had been goading Shazzan all year and as far as I was concerned the ice we had been walking on with him was thin to say the least.

I informed him that I had no intention of telling my parents, mostly because they would have been of the opinion that I probably deserved it. No, the furthest this would go would be into the school record books and we would leave it at that. He looked relieved, thanked me and I returned to the classroom via the toilets where I ran my wrists under the cold water tap to try and take the pain away.

Back in my seat Winker told me that Shazzan had been given the rest of the year off as he was suffering from stress. Yes, and no wonder. I did feel guilty about the whole thing but technically it wasn't really my fault because it wasn't me who initially shouted 'forty-five and a quarter degrees'. I shouted 'cabbage'.

That January we were invited to go on a day's skiing trip to Glenshee as guests of Knightswood Academy. Mr Menzies had a friend who taught there and I think his friend invited us to do his bit for the socially deprived.

We were to meet at the school at six o'clock on the Sunday morning as the coach was picking us up first and then off to Knightswood, which is much nearer the Highlands than we were.

We were all excited and in high spirits but totally unprepared for the weather that lay ahead. We were all in dufflecoats or denim jackets with about ten jerseys on underneath, the luckier ones also had woollen tammies and gloves.

Menzies addressed us as we approached Knightswood, 'Right, you are guests of Knightswood School and shall behave as such. I want no foul language, no threatening behaviour and no drinking. Remember you are ambassadors for your school and I want you to act accordingly. The Knightswood pupils may speak slightly differently from you but that's no reason to beat them up.'

Big Ally spoke up, 'You fuckin' sure sir?'

'Yes Dixon, fuckin' positive.'

We pulled in at the Academy and we were all taking up the whole back section of the bus and had no intention of letting anyone encroach on our turf.

The other lot got on in full skiing gear. They had the lot – suits, salopettes, jackets, gloves and packed lunches.

Winker leaned over to me, 'This lot must be loaded.'

A couple of braver ones came up to the back, noticed that Ally and Winker were occupying two seats each and asked very politely, 'Excuse me, is anyone sitting there?'

'Aye oor feet, now piss off.'

They looked a bit dejected and one bent down to whisper in Ally's ear.

Ally moved his feet and let the guy sit down, 'You tae Winker, get yer feet aff the seat and let the boy park it.'

I was puzzled until I heard the whoosh of a can opening. These two pupils had sneaked a carry out on and were sharing it with Wink and Ally.

'We didn't want to drink at the front in case Teach caught us.'

Ally said, 'Aye we cannae have Teach catching us can we?'

Ally's tone was laced with sarcasm but the guy never twigged.

The journey to Glenshee took about four and a half hours during which we tried to get to know our new companions. There were a couple of crackers amongst them and Winker and myself moved in. We shuffled up the bus and got to where they were sitting.

Winker introduced us but they just eyed us distastefully. Winker, not to be deterred, said to one of them, 'Nice anorak doll.'

'It's not an anorak, it's a ski jacket,' she said nastily.

Winker, realising that he was bombing, aimed a parting shot, 'Tell me, do you take the hand doll?'

'What!!!'

'I'm just asking ye if there's a chance of a feel behind a snow dune.'

They started calling for some guy named Kevin. Kevin duly appeared and he was a school captain type, all teeth and hairspray.

'Are these two annoying you Hazel?'

'Yes Kevin, they are being very rude.'

Kevin then said the wrong thing.

FORTY-FIVE AND A QUARTER DEGREES

'Why don't you go back and mix with your own kind.'

Winker head butted him and his nose exploded, covering Hazel in blood and snotters. Winker, satisfied that this was the Easterhouse version of a witty Noel-Coward-type comeback, left and went back to his seat to await Menzies who wasn't long in charging up the bus in a blue funk.

'Watson, what's your problem boy, don't you ever listen? That boy's nose is broken.'

'Well sir, maybe when they reset it, it'll no be as fuckin' far in the air.'

Menzies explained that Kevin wanted to press charges for assault. Now this was new to us, we never knew you could get the police to fight your battles for you. Menzies' mate came up and was about to join in the verbal barrage when Winker explained, 'Sir, we were just having a laugh and he told us to get back to our own kind, sir the guy's a snob, sir.'

Menzies' mate looked at Winker, 'He told you what?'

Menzies' mate took off back up the bus and started shouting at Kevin.

He accused him of being a snob and his remarks were only fit for the gutter. Seemed Menzies' mate was a socialist.

After Kev's nose, the ice was broken and things got much better. It turned out that Kev wasn't exactly popular amongst 'his own kind' and all through the day Winker was congratulated on his hard forehead.

We arrived at Glenshee and the conditions were perfect but the bus could only take us half way up the road to where the ski slope was and we had to disembark and walk the remainder.

As the Westwood pupils climbed off all you could hear were 'Jesus Christs' and 'Bloody hells' as the wind bit through our clothing. We had never known cold like it before. Someone asked how far would we have to walk.

'About a mile and a half.'

'How come sir? The snow here is up tae oor arses, can we not ski here?'

Menzies explained that this was not a ski run, plus the place we were to collect our skis was much nearer the top, so miserable as hell we began the trek up the mountain. Every so often we'd hear swearing as someone fell down a snow-covered hole.

We reached the top and we were issued with our ski boots, skis and sticks. The Knightswood pupils had been there before and knew the drill and had all the basics. We were a fankle of wood and metal.

We started on the nursery slopes while the real skiers buggered off for higher ground. Our instructor, a German bloke named Hans, ordered us to form a line in front of him. We were skidding about all over the place and occasionally someone would go about four yards past him before falling over.

'Dig your sticks in, ja?'

We'd never met a German before and all we knew of his race was that we'd beaten them in the War and that they always went 'Urgh' when they were shot in the *Commando* comics.

He asked us if any of us had skiied before. This question was met with either a 'Aye so we fuckin' have' or a 'Aye every winter my Da jets us aff tae St Moritz'.

He then said skiing was easy and started to teach us. Because Hans was suntanned and handsome, the girls in the group were very attentive but we 'the lads' just wanted to have a shot.

'Come on Hans can we not just try it eh?'

Hans humoured us, 'You are the smartarses ja, then please if you try.'

Ally went first with a 'nae bother boys watch this' as he shot off down the slope. He was also shouting, 'Look at me mammy I'm dancing,' when he realised that he was heading straight towards a fence.

He started shouting, 'Achtung fencen, achtung fencen,' before hitting it and flying over it, landing head first in a flurry of snow, wood and dufflecoat.

Hans skiied down to see if Ally was alright and got there as

Ally was raising himself up. He shook the snow out of his hood and walked back up towards us with his skis over his shoulders.

'Fuckin' dawdle.'

Hans looked at him.

'Now we learn how to stop, ja?'

After about half an hour he let us have our first go down the nursery slope. I looked around for Ally but couldn't see him lined up with the rest of us. I then noticed him about fifty yards away on top of this dangerously steep hill.

Hans saw him too and was shouting, 'Nein nein, you are off piste.'

Ally was shouting back, 'Naw naw, yer awright, I've only had a couple of cans,' and with that he pushed his sticks into the snow and he was off. He skied like a pro and had gone about 100 yards down the hill when it became apparent to everyone except Ally that he was heading straight into the car park. When he did notice it was far too late for him to do anything about it. He shot into the car park, missing a parked car by a few inches, before colliding slam bang centre into a minibus. He stopped dead and his tammie flew off his head and over the bus. We threw off our skis and ran down the slope to see if he was alright. When we got there he was unhurt and in an argument with the minibus driver. 'What dae ye think yer daeing parking a bus on a ski slope ya prick?'

I picked up his tammie while Hans had him by the hood of his duffle and was dragging him back up the hill.

'We see your teacher now, ja?'

Ally was screaming abuse at him, 'Aw aye and whit dae ye dae fur an encore, invade fuckin' Poland?'

As the day wore on we forgot the cold and started to enjoy ourselves. We even became sort of proficient and joined our hosts on their slope. There isn't much to skiing, you go down and walk back up. Come to think of it, skiing is boring.

Winker seemed to be falling over more than everyone else and I noticed that he always fell beside Hazel. Knocking her over then falling over himself is probably a more accurate description of events.

He would then apologise profusely, help her to her feet and give her a bit of patter at the same time. I saw she was starting to laugh at his comments and was, as they say, 'right in there'.

Eventually weary, we trooped back down the hill and onto the bus for the journey home. The pupils were now evenly distributed on the bus thanks to all the new forged friendships. Winker had Hazel sleeping on his lap; he signalled me to come over and when I got there he asked me, 'Any idea how I can get my zip down without waking her up?'

By the time we reached Easterhouse we were alone after dropping off our guests and saying our goodbyes. It was around midnight by this time and we were exhausted. Menzies stayed on the bus and he was being dropped off in the city centre. As he was pulling the bus door shut to head off, he said to Ally, 'Dixon, my office 9.15 to fill in an insurance form to pay for the dent in the minibus.'

As the bus left we could see he was laughing. Was he kidding? It turned out he was.

16

LOST

Studying for O-levels was a bind and as the school day was long enough we resented having to also do homework and would come up with elaborate excuses why we hadn't.

'Sir, the dog ate it.'

'Sir, my wee brother ate it.'

'Sir, I ate it.'

and

'Sir, an eagle swooped down and stole my school bag.'

The thing was, though, most of us ended up doing our homework in detention classes just to pass the time.

In March that year, our English teacher Mr Smart decided, for reasons unknown, to field a debating team and nominated Winker, Ally, a girl in the class called Sandra, and myself as members. None of us knew what a debating team was and in the common room we discussed it.

Ally reckoned he knew more than most. 'Aye well ye see it's like an argument sort of a thing, ye get a topic and ye argue about it.'

'Is that it then, we're in a team of arguers?'

'Aye.'

We were up against Allen Glen's, a posh fee-paying school where unless you were on a bursary, your parents would be out at least £500 a term.

The first round took place at our school and the Glenners turned up in a brand new minibus with about ten supporters and a couple of teachers doubling as judges who were supposedly neutral. Our support comprised one teacher and the jannie who was there to lock up once it was over. Desks were lined up facing each other and we sat looking scruffy opposite a shiny team in school blazers and nice haircuts.

The subject was Adolf Hitler – Lunatic or Genius. We drew the short straw and had to defend him. Ally, being our captain, had to start us off. He got up and said, 'Adolf Hitler was a genius,' and sat back down again.

The judges were a bit taken aback having expected at least a few minutes of rambling. They faffed a bit until they found the bit of paper with the Glenners captain's name on it and announced the floor was his.

He patted down his hair, got up, cleared his throat and began.

'How can my learned friend in the opposition state that the aforementioned despot was a genius? Adolf Hitler was a pathetic, mentally deranged, evil scourge of humanity . . .'

Ally broke in, 'Naw he wisnae and he wisnae a desktop either.'

One of the judges banged his gavel on the desk causing Winker, who was in the process of nodding off, to jump.

'Mr Dixon you have had your say and you are not allowed to interrupt the opening address.'

The Glenner continued.

'Hitler destroyed, Hitler murdered . . . etc . . . etc . . . etc.'

He went on for a full fifteen minutes.

My turn came and I thought I had better make an effort of some description.

'Adolf Hitler made the trains run on time and that's not easy.'

Winker whispered to me, 'That was Mussolini ya tube.'

'Was it, em well okay, let me see, Hitler's army had great uniforms, he made rousing speeches and he put that siren thing on the noses of Stukas to scare the crap out of people he was dive bombing. I mean he beat Poland in three weeks and how many folk have done that?'

As I sat down I could see Mr Smart sitting with his head in his hands.

The Glenners then went on in great depth as to why Hitler was a nutter. They had the whys, wherefores and hows and we sat not really understanding what they were talking about.

The only person in our team who spoke with any authority on the subject was Sandra who talked about the upsurge of the German economy in the thirties. When she sat down I said to her, 'Where did you learn all that?' and she told me that Mr Smart had been coaching her.

Needless to say, we didn't win the first round and Mr Smart declined the rematch, which gave them a bye into the next round.

That was the end of the debating team.

Various clubs sprang up in fifth year, not exactly clubs, more like two or three pupils having their hobby funded by the council. There was a canoeing club, a hillwalking club, a cinema club and a chess club. The chess club didn't last very long as Winker took great delight in throwing the chess pieces out of the fourth floor common room window.

We all joined something except Ally who was too busy running a book on what he called 'The Biggest Tits in the School' contest. The contenders were Angela Frame and Brenda Mathieson. Ally was trying to persuade one of their fellow female classmates to nick their bras when they were in P.E. for him to measure them so he could have an official winner. He didn't have much luck and it was only years later at a class reunion that we found out that Angela Frame was the clear winner, well she claimed she was anyway. I tried to claim my winnings off Ally but he refused to pay up saying that officially the result was unofficial, whatever that means.

Our first choice was hillwalking because it sounded easy. After all, how difficult can putting one foot in front of the other in a forward motion be?

One Sunday morning the club found itself at the base of the

hills behind Largs. Menzies was in charge and, including him, there were eight of us. Menzies was dressed like Sherpa Tensing and he spoke with great authority on the basics of hillwalking, i.e. map reading and survival, but I couldn't help noticing that all his equipment, including his map and compass, were brand spanking new.

We set off up the hill but the class Fat Boy kept lagging behind and every so often we had to stop and wait for him to catch up. This annoyed Winker tremendously: 'Can you no walk any faster ya fat prick?'

Fat Boy was too exhausted to answer him back.

We'd gone about five miles in two hours when Menzies stopped, consulted his map and said, 'There should be a crashed light aircraft here.'

Winker told him, 'Maybe the wreckage was so light it blew away.'

As no plane wreckage was apparent and Menzies looked confused, he started checking his bearings. First he'd look at the map, then at the mist covered sun, then at his compass and back to the map again.

Winker was lying on his back pulling out shafts of grass and eating them. 'We lost sir?'

'No we are not lost and stop eating the grass, sheep might have urinated on it.'

Winker added, 'Can you actually read a map sir? I think you've been watching too many movies sir.'

Menzies glared at him. Winker got up and started walking away from the party.

'Watson, where are you going?'

Winker, without turning round, said, 'For a joabie, I may be gone some time.'

We waited for Winker to return before setting off in a different direction and had been walking for a further two hours when he shouted: 'Aw come on man, that's the rock I joabied behind – we're going round in circles.'

Menzies grabbed him, 'Don't be stupid Watson.'

'Me stoopit, I'm no the one with the map.'

Menzies warned Winker what he was going to do to him back at school but Winker just laughed.

'School sir, I'd be surprised if you could find it.'

We broke for lunch and Winker nodded furtively for me to join him.

'You know what's gonnie happen don't ye,' he whispered, 'we're gonnie end up stuck up here all night, run out of food and have to eat Fat Boy like they did in that plane crash in the Andes.'

I thought this over and only ate half my packed lunch. The rest I was keeping for later.

'But Wink, how lost can ye be in Largs?'

'That prick Menzies could get lost in Safeways.'

Winker was in no mood to spend the night in the hills. 'Mr Menzies, what happens when it gets dark?'

'Watson it's only half past one in the afternoon and we are not lost we are simply off course slightly.'

As darkness fell a few hours later, Menzies admitted defeat. He told us to stay put as he was going for help. We started to collect firewood and as there was no other paper to get it going we lit the map.

Winker's attitude changed from pessimistic to philosophical.

'Aye well whit's fur ye will not go by ye. I'll bet he's planned this so he can sneak off furra bit of sheep shagging.'

'Do you think people actually do that?'

'Dunno, but these country folk have strange ways.'

The thing was, though, that we seemed to be in the middle of nowhere and had neither seen sheep nor country folk with strange ways all day.

It began to get bitterly cold and as hunger started setting in Winker eyed up Fat Boy, looked pensive for a moment then stated, 'Na.'

The other members of the group weren't coping too well and were looking a bit teary eyed, especially the two females.

I tried to allay their fears. 'Look it'll be alright, maybe we should snuggle up to each other for warmth, ye know all that body heat stuff.'

They decided against it and snuggled up to each other but it was worth a try.

'What's the time Winker?' said Fat Boy.

'How wid ah know, anyway it's your fault.'

'How?'

'Just is, right.'

Winker was just trying to amuse himself.

One of the girls suggested we have a sing song round the dying small fire but Winker was having none of it.

'Right that's it, I'm offski, I'm no' sitting here listening to these bampots singing.'

I didn't think him leaving was a very good idea. 'You'd better wait here, what if you get lost?'

'Whit dae ye mean lost, mair lost than we already are, how would that be possible, we don't know where the fuck we are so how can we get mair lost ya wank, and anyway Marco fucking Polo has probably fell doon a hole.'

One of the girl's delicate ears was not used to such language.

'Do you really have to swear?'

Winker looked at her and said, 'Aye, I fucking dae.'

'Look Wink, all I'm saying is that we'd better stay here and wait.'

'You lot can stay here and freeze if you want to but I'm off, yeez can come or yeez can stay.'

We had a quick discussion and decided to go, so our intrepid team set off into the blackness. Winker looked up to the sky.

'Right one of they starry bastards up there is the north star.'

We all looked up not exactly sure what we were looking for.

'Which one?'

'Probably, the shiniest one.'

'That one's quite shiny.'

'Okay,' said Wink, 'that one there, now Largs is on the west coast so if we keeping heading that way we'll hit civilisation, well . . . Largs anyway.'

It seemed logical so we set off in the direction we thought was west.

Fat Boy was once again lagging behind.

'Are you gonnie keep up?'

'I cannae help it.'

'Well let me put it to you this way, either you keep up or ye'll lag behind and the sheep shaggers will get ye.'

After this warning, his step quickened considerably.

We trudged on and on and on and were losing faith in Winker's northern star theory when we heard the sound of a fog horn directly in front of us.

'See,' said Winker, 'that's a fucking fog horn so we are going the right way. I'm a genius.'

We climbed one last hill and there was Largs below us in all its splendour.

It took a further forty-five minutes to reach the town and when we got there the clock on the church tower said 10.30. We walked on until we found a police station and entered to report our predicament.

Menzies hadn't shown up so it was presumed he was still wandering about on the hills. Little could be done until first light according to the cops, so they phoned the Easterhouse police station in order for them to tell our parents we were safe and we were put up for the night in the Inverclyde Recreation centre.

We were exhausted and with little thought of Menzies plight, we crashed out almost immediately.

Around 8.15 the next morning Menzies was located and when they brought him down he was a babbling frozen moron. Winker couldn't resist a dig as he sat there shivering with a blanket covering his shoulders.

'Hope you were on double time sir.'

Menzies was too cold to answer him.

Two other teachers arrived by car and one drove the minibus back to the school.

With each retelling of our adventure Winker would add bits on, but when he added on a story about how we fought off a weird hill tribe who wore blue war paint the story, and Winker, lost a lot of credibility.

17

A HIGHER CALLING

That summer I received my O-level results. I'd passed in English, Geography, Arithmetic, Biology and Chemistry. Fifth year began and I was to concentrate on four out of the five subjects for Highers. There were only fifteen pupils left from the first year intake and we were given an even smaller common room, with no telly. A situation Winker resolved by stealing the TV from the fourth year common room that we'd used the previous year. There were so few of us that the classes were now less like a class and more like one-on-one tuition.

Wilco, Ally and Winker had all stayed on, which was good because without them the drudgery would have been even more drudgerous. Drudgerous is a word. It must be because I have an O-level in English. As we were each only studying a few subjects we had lots of free periods in between classes, which we spent in the common room listening to music. We were allowed use of one of the music department's record players and we could play what we wanted as long as the volume was so low it couldn't be heard out with the confines of the room.

Technically we were supposed to use the free periods to study, but we didn't. Well, we didn't want to look like swots in front of the four fifth year girls who made up our band of brothers and sisters. Ally was into Jethro Tull in a big way and I think he was trying to set the world record for playing 'Living in the Past' the most times in regular succession. He played it so many time the Dansette was renamed the Tullsette. I was never a big fan of Jethro Tull and less of a fan after hearing 'Living in the Past' 573 times in a row. The music teacher Mr Baker did, on one visit to the common room, hear the song and said it was unusual because it had five beats to the bar. This was met with a 'Is it . . . that's great eh, five beats to the bar', because none of us knew what he was talking about.

Mr Baker visited the common room many times, for two reasons. The first to drop off classical albums because he said they would broaden our horizon, and the second was to smoke out of the window. The common room window faced away from the rest of the school and this meant he could join anyone in the fifth year who smoked out of the window without being seen by the rest of the school. Not that being seen would have really mattered because Scotland hadn't gone anti-smoking nuts in the seventies. You could still smoke anywhere. In school, in the pub, in petrol stations and leaning into prams to have a look at new borns. 'Aw yer weans lovely, dae ye think it would want a fag?'

Our last Christmas at the school approached and we had the usual rituals of the school dance and the Christmas service in front of us. There was the usual enthusiasm for the dance and usual lack of it for the service.

It was another fourth-, fifth- and sixth-year deal due to lack of pupils and all that stood between us and the dance was the prelims for the Highers.

This was the big semi-final. We did the exams and met after each subject in the common room to discuss answers. No one seemed to have arrived at any of the same conclusions.

Winker tried to alleviate everyone's disappointment explaining: 'Look it's down to the marker's interpretation in't it. Okay we might all have different sorts of answers but in a roundabout way and with a bit of the old lateral thinking, they're probably roughly nearly a' a bit the same.'

I figured that not everyone could be wrong, and I hoped I wasn't amongst those who were.

A HIGHER CALLING

As there was no point in worrying until January, I put the exams out of my mind. For this dance we were allowed to choose our own entertainment and we opted for a disco, on the condition that the DJ didn't own any Jimmy Shand records.

Being fifthies we now had our pick of the fourth-year talentio and we had our eyes on a couple of crackers. Winker reckoned that to pull these two would take a bit of Dutch courage in the shape of a bottle of El Dorado. Winker drank the full bottle and I had a capful as I was still very wary of falling face down in my own vomit and wanting to die.

The dance started at eight o'clock and Winker began tanking the bottle at 6.30, so by the time we got to the dance he had puke all down the front of his new Ben Sherman Texan shirt.

We went in and Winker draped himself over a chair. Menzies noticed him swaying while holding onto the back of it.

'Are you drunk Watson?'

Winker looked up but was too ill to speak and I had to make his excuses for him.

'No sir, he's got food poisoning,' then I added the immortal statement I was to hear many times in adult life. 'He's eaten a bad pie sir.'

Menzies greeted this with scorn.

Winker took a deep breath, 'Look Minger, piss off.'

We found ourselves outside via the fire exit in about three seconds flat and we stood in the cold air suitably confused by the quickness of our impromptu change of venue.

I spoke first.

'Aw great Winker, we'd only been in ten minutes and we never even got a sniff of the fourthies.'

The words fourthies had no sooner left my lips than we heard violent retching coming from round the corner. I wandered round with Winker hanging onto my shoulder and to our surprise we found our targets for the night on their hands and knees puking all over the ground.

One of them was crying, 'Oh God, Oh God,' and the other was

whimpering pathetically. Winker seemed to be sobering up quickly thanks to the cold air and the sight of the two fourthies.

'I'd recognise those two arses anywhere, there is a God, come on.'

We wandered up to them.

'Are youse alright there girls?'

Neither of them was capable of speech and our presence didn't really register for a few seconds. They retched violently one more time then rifted a few times indicating that their stomachs were now free of toxins.

My favourite looked at me, 'Gonnie take me hame please.'

I helped her to her feet and wiped her mouth with the lapel of her jacket, 'Look ye cannae go home in that state, I'll need to walk you about for a while until you get sober.'

'I'm no drunk, I'm no.'

'Aye sure, whatever you say doll, mon.'

Winker meantime saw his chance and whispered to me, 'I've got the key to my Da's lock up, I'm taking this one here in there until she's compis mental enough for a winch.'

We were a couple of chancers and took full opportunity of the situation and headed off in different directions.

As mine sobered up we got into a nice conversation and I decided that I liked her and would not take advantage of her being a bit on the steaming side. Winker had no such morals but he still didn't manage to lose his virginity because he couldn't go to the lock-up as there was a gang hanging around outside it drinking cheap wine. He had to put his love on hold until the next time.

In January we got our results and settled down to studying for the Highers a few months hence. As this was our last chance we did as much as we could to ensure a pass, even though occasionally we tried to find a shortcut around studying.

Macbeth was part of the Higher English paper and rather than waste months trying to work out Shakespeare's dialogue we decided to go and see Roman Polanski's film version at the

G.F.T. (Glasgow Film Theatre). Hopefully that way we'd take a bit more in. We had performed *Macbeth* in the school play but we were simply reciting it parrot fashion and not taking in a word we were saying.

We headed into town for the early Saturday evening performance. There were four of us, Winker, Ally, Wilco and myself.

We walked in and the manager stopped us, I suppose we didn't look like the normal G.F.T. punters. Generally speaking, only pseudo-intellectual-vegetarian-type people in folk-singer-style garb go to the G.F.T. to see subtitled so-called art films and analyse the movie afterwards in the cinema bar.

'Oh yes Fraser, the darkened images definitely for me portrayed man's inner fight with the recesses of his subconscious pre-pubescent memories.'

For the want of a better phrase, they all talk pish.

We didn't fit that description and the manager said to us that *Monty Python's Holy Grail* was actually on at the A.B.C. in Sauchiehall Street.

'We know Mister, we're here to see *Macbeth*.'

He let us in and stood behind us with his arms crossed for most of the movie checking that we behaved ourselves.

When the exams did come there were those who were convinced they'd pass, those who were convinced that they would not and those who would take them as they came. I fell into the last category.

The first exam was Geography and although I had paid attention in class and studied all the work notes, I was still reading my jotter on the way into the exam room. I left my books on the desk specially laid out for pupils' belongings and walked to my designated desk with my name on it.

The desks had been laid out in such a way as to keep the unruly element apart.

The Adjudicator told us to turn over our papers and commence.

I scratched my head, huffed, leaned on my elbows and

wished the two hours were over. Winker I could see was having trouble and was making 'fur fuck's sake' faces. The only pupil within whispering distance was Colin Smith who was a right Mr Swotty and he would on no account aid and abet with a bit of cheating.

Winker, it appeared, was sunk. He stuck his hand up.

'Sir, I have to go to the toilet.'

The Adjudicator looked at him with disgust and beckoned to his assistant to take Winker to the toilet and stay with him.

On Winker's return he sat down and attacked the paper with great gusto. He almost had smoke coming from his pencil. After the exam was over he told me he'd stashed his jotter in a poly bag in the cistern, went in locked the door behind him and had a quick bit of revision. The Assistant Adjudicator never suspected a thing and his toilet visit was a relief in more ways than one.

The English Higher comprised of three parts. There was the play thing, then prose and finally literature. Unfortunately for me, I hadn't really bothered to learn any prose and I was too busy doing other things to sit down and read a book. Grasping at straws, I used the words of John Lennon's 'Working Class Hero' song as prose and I made a book up. My thinking was that the exam marker can't take issue with John Lennon's lyrics being classed as prose, and he can't possibly have read every book or indeed knew of every book that ever existed so he'd never know that I was at it. The book I made up was 'written' by an Army chaplain and told of his experiences when the unit he was attached to liberated Auschwitz. I had facts, figures, dates and I waxed lyrical for the required 1000 words. I handed my papers in and hoped for the best.

The two weeks of exams passed leaving us free for the rest of the term to amuse ourselves as best we could. The common room became more of a social room where we spent our time listening to music and scanning the jobs vacant in the papers. Once a week Ally would sneak a bottle of Lanliq in and he'd share it with those who wanted.

A HIGHER CALLING

The school had provided paper, stamps and envelopes for pupils to write off for jobs and luckily for us at that time Easterhouse had been broken up into segments with areas named Easthall, Blairtummock and Lochend. The area had been what's called 'spun'. It helped because as soon as prospective employers saw the name Easterhouse on an application form the applicant was at a disadvantage. The name spinning didn't last long as it just confused people as to where they actually lived and all the sub areas returned to the Easterhouse umbrella.

For those planning a career in the civil service, i.e. Cowglen Savings Bank, the results would be very important – the higher the pass, the higher the wages. Those with good grades could become clerical officers and those who hadn't been as successful would be working under them as clerical assistants. That would have been weird having a boss who was in the same class as you.

Wilco wanted a job in Cowglen, Ally didn't care where he worked as long as he got lots of dosh for very little work and Winker and I would simply take the first job offered to us.

We became friendly with some of the teachers now that the war was over. In fact it turned out that some of them were only a few years older than us and they began telling us stories of what they got up to at school. Winker was unimpressed with this however and accused them of belting us for things they'd done themselves.

In the common room Winker took to making paper aeroplanes out of the pages of his school books and flying them out of the window. This ended abruptly when the janitor appeared in the common room with a fistful of his creations and threatening to stick them up Winker's arse. It wasn't the first time we'd been threatened by the janitor, but it was the first time he'd ever made eye contact with us. He'd never done this before and always spoke to us with his eyes firmly focused at an imaginary object about a foot to the right of our heads. The best way to describe how strange and socially awkward he was is to think

Gordon Brown in a brown janitor's coat and that about sums him up perfectly. Why he picked our last day to look us in the eye was unclear and very disconcerting.

Eventually, after passing a couple of hours being disconcerted, we got a bit bored and decided to sleep away our remaining time at Westwood by pulling chairs together to form a bed.

When the end of my schooldays came I felt quite numb and finding that I could now do exactly as I wanted was a strange feeling. I'd heard that people institutionalised for long periods always return to the only life they know back in prison or mental hospital. After twelve long years could I adjust to life on the outside?

The friends who had left in third year had seldom been seen despite promises of keeping in touch and remaining pals for life. Most of them now were nearing the end of their apprenticeships or training and were real working men and women. Some were even married. Idiotic at that age, because some of their kids are now probably older than me.

I was worried that as soon as I left I'd become a hermit as everyone drifted apart. I discussed the situation with Winker as he was having one last attempt at destroying the school television.

'How the fuck is this thing still working? I've pulled out every valve and we're still getting a bastardin' picture.'

'I don't know Wink . . . last day, eh?'

'Perhaps if I papped it out of the window.'

'I'm saying it's the last day.'

'Last day of what?'

'School.'

'So?'

'Well that's us out, into the big world, get our results, get jobs, get money.'

He pulled out a wire then punched the screen and sat down defeated.

'You know I'm gonnie miss this place.'

At last he seemed to have found my train of thought.

'I mean where else can you look up birds' kilts or stare at their diddies without getting a slap in the gub?'

The meaningful conversation ended there.

The girls in the common room were wrapping presents for the teachers as a thank you for the years given out of their lives.

Winker said to them, 'Youse are aff yer heads, they get paid to teach us.'

I leapt to the teachers' defence. 'Aye maybe so but it's a nice gesture, and some of them were alright.'

Winker softened.

'Aye Menzies was a good laugh I suppose.' That was the only time I ever heard him praise anyone, but better late than never.

The door burst open and a box appeared with Ally behind it.

It contained twelve bottles of cider he'd just stolen off a pub delivery lorry, which was a foolhardy thing to do as the pub Griers was directly opposite the police station. But despite being a blagger he at least had some sense of the significance of the day.

'Mon, let's have a drink to celebrate.'

He handed out the bottles, some declined a drink and his answer to that was, 'Don't be such a poof,' even to the girls.

'Okay, okay, best of order please, five years we've been here and at last we are free.' He raised his bottle, we raised ours. It was quite an emotional moment ruined when Ally pointed at the school captain and said, 'Don't even think about taking a slug ya prick.'

The last day came to a close and we left the girls in goodbye tears in the common room and walked through the corridor towards the main door. As we walked, we didn't converse much. We were striding along with our wee sunken chests puffed out as far as they would go. We passed the graffiti we had put on the walls, the dent in the plasterboard where Winker had bounced a first year's head, in other words our everlasting monuments, our cenotaph in memory of those who fell.

FRANKIE VAUGHAN ATE MY HAMSTER

One of the footballing adults who joined in our games when they got home from work once told me that your schooldays were the best days of your life. I was thinking now that if this prophesy was true I was looking forward to a pretty miserable existence. We went through the door and out into the playground heading for the gate. I was scared to look back in case I was turned into a pillar of salt. I heard that actually happened to someone. There was now a bit of hesitancy in our steps. I think we all felt as though we were stepping out of one world and into another and once a certain point was reached there would be no going back.

We passed through the gate and I mentally envisaged it clanking shut behind us and the school disappearing in an eerie mist as though the last twelve years had all been a dream. In that split second, twelve years of education was over. I'd spent three quarters of my life behind desks at great expense to the taxpayer. Would we be able to justify the cost by becoming responsible adults who would contribute greatly to society. Of course we wouldn't.

I left Easterhouse very soon after that for East Kilbride. My parents had got an exchange with a family who wanted to move in the other direction. So we swopped Easterhouse for Greenhills, and do you know what? I much preferred Easterhouse. It may have had its bad points but the good points far outweighed them. We had good neighbours, I had good friends, I enjoyed an interesting and happy childhood and I got a great education, albeit one that was drummed into me by teachers who, I only came to realise later, were very dedicated to their profession. They must have been to teach us properly regardless of the infantile crap we put them through. Of course, whether or not they were any good at teaching would only become clear in July when we received the results of our Highers through the post. Turned out they were.

EPILOGUE

Once I'd left Easterhouse you could count the number of times I returned to the area on the fingers of one hand. If that one hand had lost three fingers in an incident involving a machete. One of the times I did return, I was sent by the *Scottish Sun* who just happened to be my employers at the time. Prince Charles had taken the French President Jacques Chirac to visit Easterhouse to show him the urban regeneration and community spirit. Paris was having urban regeneration and community spirit problems and the Prince wanted to prove to Chirac that the British could do properly what the French couldn't do at all.

Having grown up in the scheme, I was asked to do my bit for the Entente Cordiale by showing Hearts' French goalkeeper Gilles Rousset round Easterhouse. And as it is with the tabloids, they made me dress in a French outfit, which made me look like a Le Dick. Gilles was a lovely bloke and the tallest person I've ever come across. He was like a walking Eiffel Tower. My brief was to show him the similarities between Paris and Easterhouse. This wasn't easy. I took him to the Greggs in the shopping centre and showed him the Paris Buns they had in the window, and the only tower I could think of was the huge water tower in nearby Cranhill, which is sort of nearly Easterhouse anyway. He looked suitably unimpressed. What did strike me was how friendly everyone was to him. He kept goal for a team that wasn't Rangers or Celtic and his skill must have cost the Old Firm goals. I could partly understand the people in Rangers tops who approached him for his autograph because Rangers are the Sons of William and Hearts are seen as the Cousins of William, but many, many Celtic fans in tops wanted his autograph too. Which led me to believe that they had completely forgotten about that year's Scottish Cup final where Rangers put five goals past him.

All of the people we met treated him with friendliness and respect and I was proud and thought, 'Those are my people.' Glad they never gave me a showing up. Before we left I showed him the close where I'd spent twelve years of my life. It had been 'regenerated' though and looked completely different than it did when I lived in it. The bright red sandstone block been made over into some sort of plastic toy house, but I wanted to find out if every trace of my previous life had been obliterated. It hadn't because at the back of the close on the bin shelter wall the Rikki I scratched on it with a compass in 1972 was still there. I showed Gilles and he said something in French, which I'll translate. He said, 'You can take the boy out of Easterhouse, but you can't take Easterhouse out of the boy.' I made that up, he didn't. One of the K's had faded and all that was left was Riki, so what he didn't say but probably thought was, 'You're a prick, you can't even spell your own name.'